AF512757

Demystifying Death

Every living entity that is created by nature is compulsorily subjected to two phenomena. It must perform some work to survive and in the fullness of time, must perish.

Vinod Malhotra

Demystifying Death

New Age Books
New Delhi (India)

DEMYSTIFYING DEATH

Published by
NEW AGE BOOKS
A-44, Naraina Industrial Area, Phase-I
New Delhi–110 028 (INDIA)
E-mail: nab@newagebooksindia.com
Website: www.newagebooksindia.com

ISBN: 978-81-7822-446-6

First Edition: Delhi, 2013

© Vinod Malhotra

All rights reserved. No part of this publication may be reproduced or transmitted in any form or by any means, electronic or mechanical, including photocopying, recording, or by any information storage and retrieval system, without permission in writing from the publishers.

Printed and published by
RP Jain for New Age Books
A-44, Naraina Industrial Area
Phase-1, New Delhi 110 028. India

Contents

Preface

Every living entity that is created by nature is compulsorily subjected to two phenomena. It must perform some work to survive and in the fullness of time, must perish. There is no exception to this rule and Nature is absolutely ruthless in its execution. If it were not so, the entire universe would wear a worn-out and haggard appearance.

Viewed from that perspective, death is a blessing and is essential to provide vibrant energy and youthful look to our temporary abode. Let us not get delusional with respect to the permanence of our physicality, and waste no time in achieving our dreams or the task that we set for ourselves.

Something that is present everywhere cannot be seen anywhere. Similarly, an event that happens to everyone is a non-event and yet we make much ado about it.

The only way we can live and understand our life fully, is by accepting the inevitability of death and by consciously factoring it in our existence.

Chapter 1

Death—A Myth

"Death to the body is real, everything else is a myth."

The birth and death, the two phenomena in the life of every individual create an opposite impact, and are part of that duality that characterizes every event in the universe. While these two events generate opposite emotions amongst the living, the arrival and departure of every being from this world is marked with striking similarity. A newly born comes in without any add-ons and is an utterly helpless creature. The dead too, goes away without any add-ons and has to be carried away by others.

"I am dead" is a quote that defies any form of speech and utterance, and cannot be given expression in any language across the world. It would not be correct English. Dead do not speak, and if they did, they won't be dead. Apart from certain impossible situations that cannot occur with respect to death and the dead person, there are several myths, fears, ironies, sad and comical events associated with the phenomenon of death. Human beings have, over the years unraveled several facets and mysteries of life, but death continues to be an intractable enigma which only few have understood, leave alone coming to terms with them. Those who are living must know about death, an essential part of everybody's life and that indeed, will make life worth living.

Let us begin at the beginning. Death is a fact of life, of everybody's life and is not a fiction that we read about only in books and periodicals or watch in films. It happens to all of us, to all living beings. Nor is it a mystery that needs to be solved by painstaking research and investigations. The only thing uncertain and mysterious about death though, is its timing. It arrives completely unannounced and in a large number of cases, when the living least expect it. Otherwise it is transparent, predictable and indeed, absolutely certain. There are very few events in a person's life or for that matter, in the life of all living beings that can be predicted, sans the timing with absolute certainty. Death is one and perhaps the only event that falls in this category. It is not possible to predict with absolute certainty, what all will take place in the life of a child, at the time of his birth. Horoscope of a newly born child, traditionally prepared by all parents immediately at the time of birth at best, is only a suggestive document couched in very general terms that conceals more than it reveals. No horoscope has ever dared to fix the time of death of an individual. It is not a deliberate omission, but a conscious inability of all mortals to precisely make any prediction on this subject. What profession, education, marriage, ailments, characteristics and scores of other related phenomena that he will be associated with during his lifetime may be described again in vague terms, but die he will one day can be stated without any reservation.

In fact we experience death and life everyday in our twenty-four hours cycle. Symbolically, death signifies ignorance, isolation and complete obliviousness to the world surrounding us. Every night when we go to sleep, this is exactly what happens to all of us. We become unaware and all our cognitive faculties cease to function, though temporarily. We cannot see objects, cannot hear any sound, our olfactory power is at its lowest ebb and our intellect is resting. We are lost to the world and in a mild sense, are dead. Next morning, when we wake up our vision is blurred, our thoughts are confused and our feet are unstable much like a new born. We however, quickly regain our composure and are back to life as it were. In other words, we go through the experience of death at the end of every day and the dawn heralds a new birth and a new beginning.

In fact it is possible to draw a perfect comparison of life and death with the night and day phase. A day in one's life is full of action and is mostly spent in looking after the needs of the self. This is a typical youthful and a pre-old age syndrome. Indeed, all days are more or less a repetition of the earlier ones. At the end of the day we are tired, our energy is at its lowest, our intellectual faculties are also on the wane and we desperately want to hit the bed. Denial of sleep for long hours sometimes can make us collapse. We describe ourselves as 'dead tired' and our body pleads for rest. This is the state all of us find ourselves in, during our old age. Next morning is not very different from the condition of a new born for a few moments, and we quickly recapture our stability and adulthood. Let us extrapolate a day to a period stretching to full life and we will discover striking similarities. Closer to the appointed day of death, or in other words, in old age we are quickly tired, our energy is at its lowest and we want to rest more often than we want to work. Our daily routine should give us some knowledge and experience of the phenomena relating to life and death. There is another aspect of our symbolic death and birth during the twenty-four-hour cycle. *We must temporarily experience death to be able to live fully, and properly*. For instance, if we do not get proper sleep for the prescribed period that body needs, our next day is wasted. If we do not sleep soundly, dawn looks anything but promising. In other words, if we do not die fully metaphorically, we do not live fully physically. Death therefore, is essential for us to live fully with all the required zest and energy. Everyday our sleep marks the death and decline, and the morning heralds a new beginning and, regeneration.

Let us learn to observe it closely and we would have solved the initial riddle surrounding death.

"This way perhaps, we will discover one of the easiest methods of knowing the phenomenon of death".

Death to a man is like darkness to a child. In order to understand the true meaning and implications of this statement, we have to first understand correctly the anatomy of a child. A child is an utterly helpless creature with little or no power of reasoning. He is essentially a gross physical entity with all the trappings of a living being that are highly underdeveloped. He does not possess the required discrimination to tell right from wrong, hot from cold, day from night and indeed light from darkness. He does not know that darkness is transient and shall soon be replaced by light. His helplessness is further compounded by complete invisibility of anything familiar and cessation of all functional faculties. He faces imminent death without knowing its meaning and without its actual occurrence. Hopelessness combined with absolute helplessness signals death. He needs someone to rescue him from that ordeal and left in that state for long, he will actually die. Interestingly however, as soon as light reappears, the memories of that experience will become history and he will have difficulty in recalling that experience. In other words, he will have no memories of his symbolic past life in his new birth.

Apply these two lethal combinations of hopelessness and helplessness to a grown up and you will reach the same conclusion. In real life and of course, even in a broad daylight what is that affects the dying person? He is physically a wreck, his intellectual and cognitive faculties are on the wane. There are several activities that he cannot perform without the help of others and in a sense is a burden on others. In many respects the physical and mental capabilities of a dying man and a new born are identical. Their respective look and appearance may be different, but the functional capacities would almost be similar. Let us step into the shoes of a child to correctly appreciate the state of his fragile mind and try and simulate the experience of being in complete darkness. Death would not appear any different. We need to consciously attempt to simplify the concept and notion of death and regard it as any other event in our life. Easier said than done, many would remark, but if we do not do this we will continue to lead an ordinary existence like many of our ilk and perhaps not very different from the members of the animal world and pass away completely unnoticed. We have a choice between demystifying it and understanding its correct implication, or live under its constant fear and die at the appointed time, without achieving anything worthwhile.

Unfortunately, most of us exercise the latter option. Fear of death is perennial and seldom leaves us even for a moment. Ironically, that perhaps is also the reason why our instinct for survival is the strongest instinct that we possess in our consciousness. This constant fear somehow, gets converted into an unwarranted belief that death is something that happens only to others, and we will largely remain immune to it. Strangely, our mental conditioning plants us at the end of the queue in getting affected by an event that is against our interest. Conversely, we are conditioned to be the first one to receive a windfall. This therefore, makes us weirdly complacent and we do not spend any thoughts on trying to understand it, leave alone prepare for it. This universe operates on the basis of duality and there is always a flip side to all phenomena that take place. There are some commonly used quotes, "if you want peace, be prepared for war". "Anyone who has not seen sorrow cannot value happiness". Then there are two opposites in any activity that we engage ourselves in or in the phenomena that take place, yin and yang, negative and positive energy, victory and defeat, etc. Similarly, if there is life, there has to be death. Even if we know somewhere deep within us that death will surely visit us one day, we feel inexplicably and unreasonably convinced that our time has not come and carry on regardless.

One of the first steps towards trying to demystify death and several myths surrounding it is to be fully aware of it. It need not remain in our thoughts obsessively, but somewhere in our consciousness it must be factored in as an inevitable part of our existence. This is prudence and a sign of wisdom. There are certain events in our life that may or may not occur. Some things happen only to some people and the rest either escape or are deprived. Death however, does not fall in the optional or selective category and spares no one. Lack of awareness of this fundamental fact and the assumption of immortality is a dangerous combination. This can either turn human beings into megalomaniacs or as another extreme, make them physical wrecks.

Death should be seen as an opposite of life, a phenomenon that is an integral part of the syndrome of duality that governs every aspect of our existence in this universe. Death is universal, non-discriminating and indeed, essential for the preservation of the universe in the form that is available to us all. Would anyone in a rational and sensible state, want the world to be any different than in its present form?

Chapter 2

Death—A Complete Stranger

"Death is one stranger, you need not treat with suspicion."

Some of us are perhaps familiar with the anecdote relating to the question that was put to Yudhishtar, eldest brother of the Pandavas just before the start of their journey heavenwards. Someone asked him that you have lived a very pious life all throughout, and have not willfully caused any harm to anyone. You are known to have respected life as no one has, and hence are most qualified to answer this question. Please tell us what is the most fascinating thing that you observed in your life on earth? Yudhishtar thought for a while and said the most interesting aspect of human life was that while we observe and witness the death of many, including our own friends and dear ones, for some strange reason we seem to believe that death will not occur to us. We are generally conscious of all other dualities, but the incident of death somehow escapes our perceptive nature. Fact is that all of us, including the most enlightened ones, the yogis, the most powerful and the weakest alike, will meet their nemesis at the appointed time and nothing in this universe can avert that happening. Death indeed, is a necessity, marks a renewal and hence a very desirable event in the life of every living being. In the history of mankind, indeed in the history of the entire universe till date, it has not made any exception and is not likely to, in future.

This reality need not frighten us and should perhaps make us little more sanguine. We need not wait for death with any feelings of anxiety but remain prepared and accept it as any other event of our life. Prudence demands that occurrence of an inevitable event be treated as an essential one and accepted gracefully, as and when it comes. The Gita simplifies the phenomenon of death as an act of discarding old worn out clothes and donning the new ones. It cannot get simpler than that.

In Chapter 2, Shloka 22 The Gita says:

Vasansi Jernani Yatha Vihaye
Navani Grihnati Naroprani
Tatha Sharirani Vihaye
Nyanyani Sanyati Navani Dehi

"The soul assumes a new body after the death of an old decrepit one the same way, as a person who discards old worn out clothes and puts on new ones".

A misplaced belief that death is meant for others and not for us, creates a very piquant situation when it actually strikes us or our near and dear ones. We are obviously not prepared for it. It then hits us twice as hard it otherwise would, if we were prepared and had accepted it as a likely occurrence in the lives of all of us. Awareness and knowledge of death is somewhat of a catharsis and may in some people, create a positive impact in abandoning bad habits and performing good deeds. It may not, but even if it brings about a positive change in few, it is worthwhile factoring in our thoughts. This awareness may also compel us to leave a legacy that is relatively clean and is a cause of least trouble to our descendents and heirs. In any case, a mistaken belief and willful ignorance will only lead to unmanageable grief and insurmountable grievances to all concerned.

There is also an element of gross selfishness involved in this thought. When we consider ourselves immune to death and hope that this is something that happens only to others, we are in a way, wishing it for others to the exclusion of the self. It is also equally true that our wishes in this regard are never likely to be fulfilled, but mere thought smacks of selfish and unethical conduct and is difficult to justify in any situation. Nature, like all celestial bodies, treats all living beings in an identical manner. Its benevolent and malevolent features affect everyone equally. Death is also one of the important attributes of nature which is unceasingly engaged in the task of termination and renewal, and in doing so does not act with any partisan approach. Rains and sunshine is equal to all. Nature evidently, would not allow death to have a discriminating stance.

Prudence therefore, demands that we remain aware of it, expect it to happen without waiting for it, and keep performing our prescribed Karmas to the best of our abilities. This will effectively remove any fear that we may unconsciously nurture, of an event that is an absolute certainty. We will also be in a position to ensure that we leave pleasant memories behind, and do not inadvertently become a cause of quarrels and strife over our material possessions, which necessarily have to be left behind. Some people cause happiness where ever they go, others whenever they go. Let us make sure that we do not identify ourselves with the second half of the statement.

We all have a short stay in this universe, and the only way we can make it longer at least in the thoughts and memories of others, is to perform good deeds and leave an undisputed legacy behind. No one in this world has succeeded in defying death on a physical plane, but it is possible to do so in metaphysical sense by performing good karmas that remain etched in the memory of successive generations. All great people born in this world continue to live for ever, and ordinary mortals live shorter than their actual life. Ordinary existence is a meaningless period of stay, completely unnoticed and as good as not lived. Indeed, it is an opportunity missed and lost, to move a few steps forward in our ultimate goal of realizing the truth. The scriptural wisdom opines that out of the entire living organism in this universe, human birth is a rare occurrence and becomes available only to a few on the basis of past good karmas. In that respect, it is also a subject of envy of many gods and goddesses. Do not allow it to be wasted away. Some, in fact only a few amongst us, realize this truth and use it to get closer to Him. Compare the lives of Mahatma Gandhi and millions of his followers who participated in the freedom movement. You must do something extra-ordinary to be able to defy death and the first step towards that is to know and shed your fear of it.

Having made a passing reference to our karmas of past births, let us also understand very clearly that this is not the end of our existence in this universe. Our real self is not the body as majority of us tend to believe. Our body is subject to decay and decline because of an overdose of excessive indulgence combined with normal process of ageing and gets dissolved into the same matter that it comes from, overtime. Our real self is our Atma, soul that is eternal and a representation of the Supreme energy and in course of time, gets another body depending again upon our karmas. Krishna, in Chapter 2, Shloka 12, tells Arjuna that he is not meant to suffer only one birth. The context is the Mahabharata war, where Arjuna seeing his own kith and kin arraigned against him, refuses to fight and become the cause of their death.

Krishna then elaborates on the concept of birth-death cycle of all living beings and says:

Na Tvevaham Jatu Nasam
Na Tvam Neme Janadhipa
Na Chaiv Na Bhavishyama
Sarve Vyam Mata Param

"In the cosmic context, there was never any time when I was not present, or you and all these kings and warriors were not present. In future again, all of us would remain in this universe".

Therefore, who are you grieving for?

We need to know and understand that we are a microcosm of this macro energy that rests comprehensively in the owner of this universe. Some of us call Him God and some associate Him with Supreme energy. That is eternal and cannot possibly have any short term existence. In the same logic, we, as an integral part of that entity are also eternal, and the only way our existence is obliterated is when we merge into that entity. Our physical death or the death of a body does not mark the termination of our being. It only marks a temporary interregnum between two physical births.

Avyaktadini Bhutani
Vyaktmadhyani Bharat
Avyakt Nidhnani Aiv
Tatra Ka Paridevna

Krishna tells Arjuna in Chapter 2 at Shloka 28 that all living beings remain in an unmanifested form before their birth and after their death. They become visible, only during the period in between and hence he should have no cause for sorrow.

Humans are spiritual beings with a physical experience and, are not mere physical beings with a spiritual experience.

The spiritual experience referred to above can not be to a body that is subjected to decay and renewal. It must necessarily to an entity that is constant and perennial. It should also be pure and pristine. We have heard of that entity and in common parlance, all of us describe it as 'soul'. The soul has several epithets given to it by different people, depending upon their understanding of this entity.

The Gita unequivocally recognizes its permanence and indestructibility in Chapter 2, at Shloka 23 as follows:

Nainam Chindanti Shastrani
Nainam Dahti Pawaka
Na Chainam Kledyantyapo
Na Shoshayati Maruta

"The Soul can not be pierced by any weapon, fire can not burn it. It can not be dissolved by water, nor can it be dried by air".

Krishna, in shloka 24 and 25, further describes Soul as everlasting, something that is present everywhere, absolutely stable and completely unchangeable. In other words, it possesses all the attributes that we visualize in the Supreme power, Parmatma. Our soul has another very interesting characteristic. It is absolutely indifferent to all actions that we perform during the course of our journey in this world and most importantly, it is absolutely immune to the phenomenon called death.

Death therefore is only to the body, which in any case is made up of organic substances that are present everywhere in this universe. Human body and indeed, the bodies of all living beings in varying degrees are composed of what is commonly described as 'Panchbhuta'. The famous five elements such as fire, earth, water, air and ether (it represents the sky) are the main components of our body, and in them it dissolves at the end of its tenure. Interestingly, all that a body has is available in abundance in the universe. You need a master craft person to put them in right compositions and you get a human being, an animal, a bird and a whale, if you please. The only catch however is, that master is extremely elusive, unreachable and does not belong to any mortal class. Nature, be profusely thanked for this dispensation or else there would be absolute chaos in this universe. One shudders to imagine a situation if some mortal being is entrusted with this task. His vulnerability and amenability to undue influence will make corruption a cosmic phenomenon, and cause havoc with respect to the incidents of life and death. Some people have tried in vain to play God and some others will again make an attempt to do so. However, this is one area of great specialization that one hopes and believes, will continue to remain outside the competence and jurisdiction of ordinary mortals. Any other situation will be absolutely disastrous.

All human beings are imperfect. The greatest of the people born in this world at any time of the history had some weakness. I dare some one to suggest the name of a person who at any stage of his life did not do anything wrong, or did not entertain evil thoughts. Some highly enlightened people may have lived their life in an absolutely impeccable manner, doing nothing that can be faulted with, or doing nothing that is visibly or tangibly wrong, but there is no one who would not have entertained some negative thought or desire, at some stage of his life on earth.

The Gita says that nature has designed all living beings in such a way that each one is influenced by a combination of three Gunas, namely satvik, rajsik and tamsik. The proportion of these Gunas may vary and the prevalence of one largely creates the general image of a person in society. In Chapter 18, Shloka 40, it says:

> *Na Tadasti Prithivyam Va*
> *Divi Deveshu Va Puna*
> *Satvam Prakriti Jairmuktam*
> *Yadebhi Syat Tribhirgune*

> *"No one in this world, not even gods in heaven are free from the influence of these three Gunas that have been created by nature".*

The only entity that is presumed to be perfect is that Supreme energy or power that controls this universe and its creation. He is beyond and above all Gunas and nature. He is absolutely impartial, equal to all, is present everywhere and is completely invulnerable. He is not amenable to any pressure or prejudices. He is the only one who has all the attributes, qualifications and experience of a master craftsman, referred to above. The task of creation and destruction, of life, death and renewal has to be in the hands of that perfect entity and none else.

Our real self is the soul and that represents our real identity. The body is just an outer covering that is subject to decay, death and subsequent renewal. This covering needs regular replacement and in the absence of any suitable definition, we call it death. Death, in no way marks the termination of our identity. In fact, it marks a much needed renewal and continuation of energy in a kinetic form. This entire phenomenon is controlled and operated by an entity that is absolutely perfect and impartial.

CHAPTER 3

Fear of Death

> ***"Fear of any kind is debilitating and must be consciously avoided."***

"I will kill you" is the ultimate threat that a man can hold for another of his ilk. The objective is to create the greatest of fears in the mind of an opponent or an enemy, and force him to behave in a manner that is entirely agreeable to the aggressor. The generation of a partial fear may at best be achieved by threatening to break a leg or by damaging the material ownership, but an absolute fear would demand nothing less than the threat of a death. The reason for this is not difficult to discover. Human beings, for that matter no living being can see anything beyond death. This is the end of the road, a cul-de-sac. If there is anything, it is only a narrow and deep precipice which again signals death.

It is extremely strange though, to accord a higher level of fear to death, in comparison to the acute pain one is likely to suffer on multiple fractures or the loss of a leg or two. Death indeed, would mean instant cessation of all pain, while the loss of a vital limb means an extended phase of excruciating pain which is further compounded with intense misery. It may be interesting to understand the anatomy of fear before fully establishing its correlation with the phenomenon of death.

Fear is a product of complete lack of courage. Lack of courage in general, lack of courage in one's convictions and intellectual dishonesty, are more or less synonymous terms, and have their origin in selfish desires and a sense of fear. Let us first discuss the anatomy and the psychology of Fear.

Fear is one of the many primordial emotions present in all living beings since the beginning of civilization. Fear of death is of course the ultimate fear and all other fears are present at different rungs of the ladder, depending upon the perception of the person affected by them. In the early days, man was scared of absolute loneliness and natural disasters that used to occur frequently and, in the absence of any knowledge about such phenomena, he would get frightened. There were very few means of protection against nature and wild animals, and he remained constantly under threat to his life. Survival continued to remain a major challenge till by his ingenuity and persistence, he managed to tame various forces that held a potential threat to him. This was also the period when several superstitions came to play a significant role in the lives of people, particularly about the events of which they had no knowledge, or over which they had no control.

Sadly, some of these superstitions still persist. The sense and the extent of fear gradually started abating as science and technology progressed, and human beings got greater control of natural events and managed to create several means of protection against nature, wild animals and man-made threats. In other words, the external factors that generated a sense of fear have been more or less accounted for and humanity is today much better prepared to handle these crises. It is however not possible to say that man has conquered all. Nature is far too powerful and some natural events of gigantic proportions can still play havoc with life, over which man has no control. That is why it is extremely important to respect nature and not mindlessly exploit natural resources out of greed. The reference is to the issue of massive environmental degradation that we have caused to our planet and are still persisting in this ruthless occupation regardless of impending disaster. Not content with polluting the earth, we have set our sights on other planets of our solar system, which once conquered will perhaps face the same fate.

The psychology of fear in the modern context has of course taken a slightly different form. So far we have talked about the concept of fear at a macro level. It is equally important to talk about its psychology at a micro level, something that affects us on a regular and an immediate basis. Fear is such a powerful negative emotion that not only does it make us intellectually dishonest it forces us to borrow the courage of others' convictions rather than our own, and renders us thoroughly dispirited. Fear enters our system because of the following reasons:

1. We have lied to others who are important to us.
2. We have committed a crime and there is fear of getting caught. If we do not get caught in a reasonable period of time after the detection of crime, this sense of fear starts declining.
3. We have fears for the safety and security of self and our close ones in that order.
4. Fear of losing near and dear ones, or a precious possession.
5. Fear of our expectations and desires, not getting fulfilled.
6. Even after getting our desires fulfilled, the fear of losing them. We want to hang on to them for ever.
7. The fear of authority.

8. Fear of losing our good name and reputation, built over several years of hard work and service.
9. Fear of losing in any competitive situation, in a game, in sports, in a class-room test, etc.
10. Fear of one's own death.
11. Lastly, the fear of God, this though exists only semantically and does not normally, deter people in doing what they want to do.

We, at this point need to distinguish "desirable fears" from the "undesirable ones".

The list is only illustrative and there may be several other minor worries that may not qualify as fear.

Telling a lie or committing a crime, are obvious causes of fear, because they entail immediate and sometimes severe punishment, when caught. A lie does not have any basis for existence and sooner or later, it is exposed and depending on the damage it has caused, it normally invites censure or punishment. Unfortunately, in a society where crime detection and its prosecution are lax, the extent of fear is less and the incidence of crime is heavy. Expeditious disposal of crime cases not only engenders necessary and desirable fear, it is also an effective tool for controlling crime. Usually, criminals start with petty crimes and if not caught in the early days, get emboldened for more heinous ones. These are a few categories of fears that are desirable in any civilized society otherwise there would be a total chaos.

The fear of death is a syndrome which is all-pervading. It affects everyone, even the most intrepid amongst us, and has to be discounted as a common denominator. Nobody has escaped it yet and is not likely to ever do so in the future. In fact, in certain ways, it is desirable to leave this decrepit body after a period when it starts becoming an encumbrance rather than an aid. But however ramshackle we become, the desire to keep on living for ever never leaves us and hence, we constantly fear the arrival of death. However the fact of its universality and certainty should help us come to terms with it.

The Gita talks of a very profound and well-known truth in Chapter 2, Shloka 27:

Jatasya Hi Dhruvo Mritu
Dhruvam Janam Mritasya Cha
Tasmat Apariharthe
Na Tvam Shochitum Aharsi

"Death to those who are born is a certainty and those who die shall be born again. Nobody can do anything about this phenomenon. It is pointless therefore to either grieve or fear death".

Death is a renewal, a renaissance and for the person dying a process of refurbishing his worn out physical assets and, indeed, nothing more. He does not die, nor does his Atma perish but only seeks renewal, like replacement of an old part. We in this world have unnecessarily romanticized the incident of death by our silly attachments to worldly objects and people. We cry, scream and exhibit such insane behaviour on the termination of ephemeral objects and beings as if there is no tomorrow.

Let us for a moment patiently analyze the anatomy of our sorrow, on the occasion of the death of near and dear ones. Firstly, let us see it from the point of view of the person dying. Taking the law of averages, death usually strikes at a ripe age, unless some serious affliction hits a person. That person has lived his life and is usually over the hill and on the decline.

His body functions have also started diminishing and it becomes difficult, if not impossible, for him to lead a full life. His death is also a certainty. All these factors are indeed conducive for him to make an honourable and dignified exit, without becoming too much of a burden on others. Is it not a great way to leave this world?

Now for those left behind, their turn would also come in the fullness of time. They however choose to express their grief by shedding tears and showing insane behaviour in utter disregard of the condition of the departed. They perhaps cry for two reasons. They cry because they loved the dead person immensely and in his absence would feel deprived and lonely, or they wish to tell the world how sad they are at the departure of that noble soul. Both reasons smack of selfishness and must be quietly disapproved. Interestingly, that person over whom we grieve, has no perception of those who grieve. Crying over anyone's death therefore, is an exercise in utter futility.

There is an important lesson to be learnt. Let us not fear death but keep doing our jobs in accordance with our capabilities. Expect it to happen, prepare yourself for it so that you do not become the cause of strife and misery after you are gone.

The class of fear that is eminently undesirable and which we need to discard is of a completely different hue and shape. It stems from our unfulfilled desires and unbridled greed for material acquisitions. This phenomenon is also a breeding ground of increasing intellectual dishonesty in all spheres of our interpersonal relationships. Most of our fears in day-to-day dealings are directly linked to our desires. We desperately want certain things to happen and there are invisible forces at work. The fear will keep haunting us till that thing happens in our favour. You want an out-of-turn promotion in your organization. Pending that, you will be careful not to displease your boss. In fact, you will do everything possible to please him including indulging in acts that smack of blatant intellectual dishonesty. Usually, the impact of fear would be much greater if the desire that one nurtures is either premature or unreasonable.

Even after acquiring the object of our desire, the fear factor lingers on. Now the problem is not its acquisition but a fear of the object being taken away. Again, the fear quotient would be bigger if that object has been acquired by unfair means or one is not actually deserving of it. The best policy is to remain perpetually sanguine, always cheerful and confident about the future and get out of the bondage of all forms of dualities. The conflict of extreme emotions swinging from one end to another like a pendulum can be very debilitating. It is best to remain in a state of Samta or what is described as a Samatva Bhav. If you get what you are waiting for without going overboard, you should be content. If you do not get it, even then you should be content. My experience is that what belongs to you will come to you sooner or later, and that which does not belong to you will elude you, no matter how much you fret or fume over it. It actually never belonged to you. In this condition the fear psychosis of not getting something or losing it, will cease to torment you.

One of the serious mistakes that parents commit in bringing up their wards is to instill in them, a desire not only to excel but be the best in whatever they do. The standard refrain in most households is to win and 'come first'. Now we all know that it may not be possible always. We do not realize the pressure it creates in the little minds and it is not always possible for him to live up to the expectations, particularly of his parents in all spheres of activity. He carries that guilt all his life and this cumulatively can develop into suicidal tendencies. The fear of 'coming second' or being relegated to a place way down the ladder can be debilitating.

I recall my own childhood. I was better than my siblings in studies but certainly not the best in the world. But the pressure created by my parents and relatives would make me utterly miserable, and on the day results were declared in school, I would wait for the announcement with bated breath. More often than not, I would be placed second or third leading to a prolonged phase of utter misery and depression. Thankfully, I learnt to reconcile with my limitations in later life and no longer experienced any hurt or deprivation in the event of getting less than expected. Now there is also an intelligent realization that there are others in this world who indeed are, and can do, better than me. I am responsible only for my work and the results are in the hands of others. This is also consistent with the oft-repeated dictum of the Gita not to ever get attached to the result of your actions.

Leave alone the fear of losing it is actually good to lose once in a while. Winning ceases to teach, makes you complacent, stops growth of any kind and in more cases than one, makes you arrogant. Our society, however, places a premium on winning and indeed glorifies it. Often it happens that both winner and the loser cry in front of the crowd, of course for different reasons. To be able to understand the worth of winning, it is important to lose once in a while or else you stagnate. Also, usually it is the loser who actually keeps moving ahead and not the winner.

There is an interesting anecdote from the tales of Shiva and Parvati, the manifestations of Purusha and Prakriti. Shiva by Himself is inactive, a dead body (*Shava*). In order to infuse life in this dead body, Parvati, the Prakriti, has to play with it, without merging into it. Parvati must necessarily keep Shiva in an awakened state and keep playing with it to keep the cycle of creation and destruction going. While playing, she also has to keep winning and losing. In fact, she has to keep winning more often than not, resulting in Shiva losing most of the time. The reference is to the game of dice, introduced to the couple by the celestial bard, Narada, and the wager is a hug. If Shiva wins, he gets to hug Parvati and assumes a state of Ardhanareeswara, the androgynous two-in-one form. If that happens, however exciting and beautiful it may seem, he reaches a state of complete inactivity which effectively means the end of the world. The cycle of creation and destruction, which in the context of cosmic phenomenon represents 'renewal', ceases to operate, definitely not a desirable outcome. Although losing perpetually causes immense anguish and humiliation to the supporters of Shiva, a supreme being, He continues to lose in the larger interest of maintenance of the universe in its current state.

This is how life should be led, losing and winning to ensure togetherness. This phenomenon creates several perspectives and is an important learning curve, allowing us to lose gracefully and accept success with great humility. No one in this world has won all the time. In other words the best of people in their respective fields of excellence have also failed. Don Bradman, an all time great cricketer, got out on a duck in his last innings. Nearer home, Sachin Tendulkar again one of the greatest cricketers the world has known, has failed with the bat on more occasions than one.

Let us therefore completely banish the fear of losing and prepare ourselves for the next battle that is lurking around the corner. Here again, do not fear losing. You might end up serving a much larger purpose losing than winning, and at the same time continue to work harder and living well.

In conclusion, a person with no wants or desires has no worries. None of the fears described above bother him and he remains free of all bondages. A classic case, though extreme in nature, relates to Swami Vivekananda. When he left the shores of India to attend the Parliament of World religions in Chicago in 1893, he did not have a penny in his pocket. He did not carry a passport or any other proof of identification. He also did not carry any fear with him. Some of us may be familiar with the story that at the end of that conference, people of America were eating out of his hand. Such was the force of his magnetic personality, his oratorical skills and a complete absence of fear.

Let us look at three Shlokas of Chapter 16 (1, 2 and 3) of the Bhagwad Gita that describe the attributes of a person with a divine nature or, shall we say, an ideal human being:

1. *Abhayam Satva Sanshudhi*
   Gyan Yoga Vayavasthiti
   Danam Damasch Yagayasch
   Swadhaya Tap Arjavam

2. *Ahimsa Satyam Akrodha Tyaga*
   Shanti Apeshunam
   Daya Bhuteshu Aloluptvam
   Mardwam Hrir Chapalam

3. *Teja Khshama Dhriti Shoucham*
   Droho Natimanita
   Bhavanti Sampadam Daivim
   Abhijatasya Bharata.

Three compositions outlined above state the qualities that are desirable in an individual. These are:

- Absence of fear, purity of heart
- Cultivation of spiritual knowledge

- Charity, sense-control, sacrifice
- Study of scriptures, austerity, virtue
- Non-violence, truthfulness
- Absence of anger, renunciation
- Tranquillity, aversion to criticising others
- Compassion, freedom from greed
- Gentleness, modesty, determination
- Courage, forgiveness, fortitude
- Cleanliness, freedom from hatred

These are twenty five attributes Krishna spells out that are desirable in an ideal human being. To find all these qualities in one person is a near impossibility. Interestingly, the first quality that Krishna recommends relates to absence of fear, *Abhyam* and not fearlessness. There is no point boasting of fearlessness and go to a forest to start a duel with a lion. The lion is obviously going to eat you up. The absence of fear in this example would mean that if you come across a lion in a forest, you do not panic and stand your ground. In all likelihood the lion would quietly or at worst, disdainfully ignore you and walk away. Fearlessness might make you take on the lion headlong and we can guess the outcome. The important thing is to make an honest assessment of your own strength, use your cognitive faculties and lead a life free of fear, and other negative and dangerous emotions.

There is another noteworthy feature of the several qualities enumerated above in the three Shlokas. As mentioned earlier, it may be too much to expect from us mortals, an assimilation of all the qualities in one go. If you tell yourself that I am going to pick up just two or three of these habits and follow them to the hilt, you will in time discover to your surprise, that you cannot but help imbibe many of them, if not all. The preponderance of a few good traits will by themselves, make you a highly respected person in the eyes of others.

The detailed description of the anatomy and psychology of fear in effect can be summed up in one sentence.

The perception of a loss of our material possessions including our body and the threat of pain, in fact the anticipation of pain are the primary, and perhaps the only ingredients of fear.

Recently, I had an occasion to travel to Spain with my family and during the course of our journey we spent two full days in Barcelona, a lively bustling city of international repute. Olympics held in this city few years ago, lent it a character of a world class metropolis with a state-of-art infrastructure that was aesthetically superimposed on its Catalonian historicity. Its sylvan grandeur and beauty had also attracted large number of beasts in the form of criminals and pick-pockets. I unwittingly became a victim of one of their class, who with sheer adroitness managed to relieve me of my bulging purse that had a fortune in terms of cash and several cards, including the proof of my identity. Our holiday had just begun and we had planned for another ten days stay in Spain, including five days in a cruise. Before this young man most skillfully divested me of my precious belongings, I nursed a fear. Fear of losing the support system for our holidays, from which there was no going back, was a little unnerving. It completely disappeared after that. I was a free man and do not remember having enjoyed my holidays like I did during the remaining part of my tour.

I had nothing to lose and the perception of any loss had completely vanished. The most delectable recipe of living one's life to the fullest and enjoying every moment of it lies in seeking, absolute freedom from any kind of fear. Those who have managed to conquer the fear of death, the ultimate fear, lead a complete and meaningful life. All the rest of us merely exist.

In the foregoing description of the anatomy of fear, we have seen some distinction between desirable and the undesirable fears. This distinction is however only semantic in nature. In real sense all fears are crippling and unnecessary and must be consciously jettisoned from our psyche. We may also observe that majority of fears that affect us are caused by some action on our part, or on account of an event in which we have some role to play. If these actions are not performed, or if that event does not take place, the cause of fear also disappears. Interestingly, the event of death is one in which we have no role to play. Why should that generate any fear? It is not logical and indeed, is wholly irrational therefore to nurse any fear of death.

To conclude therefore, the incident of fear, if any, should be restricted only to what we do or do not do, during our lifetime and not to the incident of death or its anticipation. In other words, the only thing we need to fear is our own evil nature, bad karmas and our negative emotions that propel us to act in an undesirable manner.

CHAPTER 4

Our Fragile Existence

"Everything outside of us is hostile.
Strength has to be found within."

All living beings in this world are designed with two distinct components and each of these have an assigned role. There is the subtle, psychological part and the gross, which is the physiological. Human beings in particular, have a body made up of natural elements and it also has perceptive capabilities stored in its subtle components. We need to dissect it further. The gross part of human beings comprises the body as a whole with certain mechanical parts such as, head, arms, feet, eyes, ears and other vital organs, some visible and some not. The subtle components consist of intellect, mind, senses, foresight etc.

Our contact with the external world is essentially through our senses. The next level is that of our mind, and our senses have both a symbiotic as well as an empathetic relationship with our mind. Our intellect housed in the safe environs of our brain, operates at a higher level and lends us the power of discrimination and memory. Of course, it has other allied functions such as analytical ability, vision, imagination and power of retrieval of stored information. It is another matter that some of these functions are never used during our lifetime. Our intellect is the only entity that can exercise some control over our wayward sense-mind combination. Then, there is an entity called ego that is present in some measure, in all of us and plays a vital role in shaping up our general standing in society. Some people call ego as an entity which is a necessary evil. Our real self however, is none of these described above and that is, our soul. Everything else except the soul is perishable, and are subjects that are very dear to the phenomenon called death.

It would be interesting to examine the process of evolution from the stage of a new born to old age and death, and the corresponding role and functions of the physiological and psychological features present in our system. It is extremely important however, to understand that at every stage of our growth and journey from womb to the grave, both these features, the subtle and gross are present, albeit in varying degrees.

A new born is essentially a bundle of flesh and blood and all other features that make him look human. He is primarily a body, predominantly physiological, gross with a modicum of subtlety that is just about sufficient to survive in alien surroundings. All his five senses are functional but those that are critical for his survival, are more active than others. For instance, the sense of touch, breathing and hunger are more pronounced than his vision and hearing. He is very little brain and little or no intellect at this stage. This however, must change and before long all his senses are in full flow. A few years down the line, he starts showing his mind and indeed, starts expressing it. The intellectual component is still conspicuously absent but not for very long. In fact, in some children described as child prodigies, the intellectual quotient sometimes overrides the mind power.

The body growth picks up and very soon reaches a state when it starts moving about at a speed much faster than most of us can cope with. He acquires youthfulness and is full of energy that is marked by physical strength and vitality. Some parents describe their children as hyper and find difficult to cope up with their boundless energy. The emphasis is still primarily on the gross and the subtle component is essentially in a receptive mode, more than being reactive. The mind and intellect is observing, absorbing and storing all his experiences in the sub-conscious. This is a critical stage of a child's growth and development. All his senses, mind and intellect that are in a receptive mode, form strong tendencies which in time assume the status of habits that stay with him for rest of his life. A sense of fear, or shall we say, several kinds of fears also get deeply embedded in his psyche and manifest themselves on different occasions later in life, and bear a close resemblance to the experience that had caused fear in its incipient stage. In other words, we can trace back the cause of practically all kinds of fears to an experience in the early part of our growing phase. This therefore, has lot to do with our upbringing which most parents either do not realize or even if they do, ignore it as an easy way out. At this stage of our evolution, while the body is getting stronger the mind and intellect is still weak and impressionable and all kinds of fears, real or imaginary find a comfortable parking place.

I remember the stories of ghosts, cops and dacoits and threats held out to me in my childhood, if I did something or desisted from doing something. I have not got over the imaginary apparition lurking somewhere in a room upstairs and hate to go there alone. The genesis of a large number of fears that most of us nurture, can be traced back to similar incidents in early part of our physical growth. Most parents who are generally responsible for the upbringing are either unaware or ignorant of this important fact.

Parents have an important role to play in the formation or absence of an emotion called fear, and equally important responsibility to ensure that a child poised to become an adult is equipped to dismiss all these fears as absolute rubbish. The phenomenon of fear is largely mental and emotional and a weak mind will always remain fear-ridden. Parents have to set an example of fearlessness, as also make every effort to disabuse the fragile mind of a child, from the existence of any such phenomenon. Interestingly, all fears including those that constitute a threat to our body or those that are likely to cause physical pain, impact our mind and intellect. Memories of that experience will recur at all stages of our subsequent life. It is therefore essential to treat them as non-events in the early part of a child's growth.

> *I know many friends and relations, apparently very strong and sensible, who quiver at the thought of getting a prick of an injection. They jump like a frightened Asian Gibbon before allowing a harmless and relatively painless needle, lasting a nanosecond to enter their strong body.*

Body witnesses a rapid growth and so does our mind and intellect in the next phase of our existence, and all our experiences hereinafter affect our conscious mind as against the sub-conscious state which was more pronounced in the early part of our growth. It is however, important to understand that the perception of fear and its recurrence is the product of the sub-conscious mind. The fear factor is considerably diluted, if not altogether obliterated as we grow. More importantly, as our mental and intellectual faculties become more aware and rational, the fear component starts receding. Education, knowledge, science and real-life experiences help us to understand the irrationality of fear and we are in a better position to counter it. A cursory examination would tell us that every kind of fear is irrational and as mentioned earlier, a product of our own act of omission and commission. All our actions committed in the state of complete awareness will completely neutralize the impact of fear. This phase of our life, with complete balance of physical and psychological conditions is not only most productive, it is also the most rational and hence best qualified to handle all fears. It is interesting to note that all spheres of activities which are physically challenging and have maximum risk to life and body, are performed during this phase.

Mention must however be made of another kind of peculiar fear that also has its origin in our growing up phase. Reference is to the fear that is generated by superstitions. Surprisingly, some of the fears that grow out of a completely irrational phenomenon called superstition stay with us for our entire life. They are usually passed on to us by our parents, grand-parents as heirlooms. Science, rationality, education and even awareness does not seem to neutralize fears that have superstition as its genesis. Daughters would normally desist from doing certain very sensible acts because their mothers did not do them. At some stage of their personal experience, they seem to connect an unfortunate incident with what they may have done or not done. This therefore becomes a superstitious precedent that every family member is cautioned about. There are some superstitions that are general in nature and have a universal application, like changing your direction of travel, if a cat-a black cat crosses your chosen path. Soiling your hands with ink augurs well for you in your examination. Thankfully, ball-point pens are now allowed and extensively used in examinations and hence, this superstition has become obsolete or in fructuous. There are others that are applicable, strictly to a family or clan because some peculiar incident may have taken place some decades ago that affected a member of the family. Superstitions are often linked to an accident or death in a family on certain dates or on occasions that remain etched in our memory for long.

Fact however, remains that all superstitions without exceptions are irrational, illogical and need to be rubbished unequivocally, and any sense of fear, associated with them should be completely jettisoned.

As mentioned earlier, most of our fears and their expression stem from the sub-conscious, and as a reaction to some past experience stored in there. When similar circumstances revisit us, we react more or less in the same manner as we had when they originally occurred. Some of us, in a state of relative maturity are able to effectively camouflage our reaction, but the perception of fear does affect us adversely. This is where the role of awareness becomes important. We get startled only in the state of unawareness and getting startled will inevitably be accompanied with or followed by fear. Remaining in the state of complete awareness has several other advantages and absence of fear, definitely is one of them.

Awareness, or shall we say our alert consciousness is the most effective antidote to all negative impressions that are stored in our sub-conscious.

The psychology of fear has strong relationship with elements of surprise and anticipation. Most of us spend much of our time in an anticipatory mode. We keep several desires in our bosom all the time, and this creates a kind of anticipation. Will it happen or will it not? Both forms of anticipation generate fear in our heart. We want certain events or things to happen, keep worrying over them and the possibility of their not happening creates fear. Alternatively, we do not want certain things to happen, and their likely occurrence and anticipation causes another kind of fear. Fear as an emotion, in these cases, can start affecting us well before its likely occurrence. Anticipation of any kind, especially of an unpleasant event is crippling and must be shaken off completely from our thoughts. Many parents in India for example, start worrying over the marriage of their teen aged daughters, a decade before that event is likely to take place. It is prudent therefore to inculcate a habit of crossing the bridges when we come to them.

Fear of death also hits us in an anticipatory mode. In fact, death as an inevitable event does not create any problems because it really marks the end of all sensations. It is the 'wait and anticipation' of the event that causes all consternation and fear. Interestingly however, death comes unannounced and hence even the anticipatory fear is also unfounded.

A large number of us often become victims of a surprise factor. This usually happens when others create certain situations for us, and not expecting them to occur in the manner they are thrown at us, we express great surprise. This universe operates in accordance with its own laws and rules, and many of which are not known to us. Different people act in a differentiated manner and it is not possible to understand every conduct and behaviour that causes certain action and reactions. Axiomatically speaking, if something can happen, it will happen, it is only a question of time and hence there is no place for any surprises. Cut out the surprise elements from life and you will notice that half of our unfounded fears are gone. All surprises are irrational and affect only a highly immature mind.

Swami Vivekananda, before leaving the comfortable confines of his father's house and stepping into the world on his own, asked his father for one advice that he would want him to remember all his life.

His father, a man of few words asked him not to be surprised by anything in this world and live his life on his own terms. He followed this advice to the hilt till his last breath.

Old age perhaps is the most exciting period of one's life in the context of fear phenomena, including the capacity to deal with death. Although, no one believes that he is going to die too soon, yet its awareness is more pronounced in old age vis-à-vis other phases of our existence. Intellectual faculties are also on their peak and one is now more reason and less superstition. The depleting physical strength and energy also ensures that we do not perform acts that have strong risk elements, thus increasing the probability of longevity. The fear of death is not altogether missing, but its proximity makes us more sanguine. There appears a perceptible decline in the energy and the physical strength and consequently bigger involvement in activities that remain largely in the province of the mind and intellect. The element of fear with respect to death does not disappear, but is tempered with the thought of having lived one's life and a degree of reconciliation with its imminence. Baring few exceptions, most of the universally celebrated works requiring high degree of intellectual content, have been delivered by people in their old age. Great scientists have peaked and created their path-breaking inventions usually at a ripe old age.

To the physiological and psychological components of all living beings, one needs to add one more dimension. That is the existence of Atma, the soul which represents the imperishable part of that being. Death takes place to the body, physiological which also includes the brain, heart and other vital organs. These are the most fragile part of every being. The mind, intellect and Atma that are the subtle components of living beings, remain unaffected. Our bodies are the most vulnerable part of our existence on this planet and do not possess any free or independent will. They really are a function of our Karmas, both in form and the character they assume during the course of their existence in the world. Our body indeed, is the weakest and the most fragile of all our assets. The fear of death to the body may therefore be caused by the following factors:

1. An impression that death will be preceded by intense and unbearable pain. We experience several minor and major pains during our life, but the anticipated pain of death, increases our fear manifold.
2. Threshold of our tolerance is extremely low. As our comfort levels start growing bigger, our tolerance levels start decreasing in inverse proportions.
3. To all of us, death marks the termination of our being, our identity and this creates unwanted anxiety and helplessness.
4. The fear of the unknown constantly gnaws at us, and remains with us till the occurrence of that event.

Perception of pain which is largely physical in nature therefore, becomes the central feature of our fear of death. We must examine the absurdity and utter futility of our behaviour in these situations. It is accepted that pain of any kind is dreaded and we mistakenly believe that death, an ultimate destruction of the living being must mean bigger pain. On the contrary, death signifies cessation of all pains. Even any sensation of pain immediately preceding the death, is much less than several other pains that we experience during our life-time. Pain caused by a phenomenon called migraine, pain in the regions of stomach caused by intestinal infection, pain occurring on suffering a fracture in the bones and even ordinary muscular pain cause much bigger trouble. The pain caused by dishonour or on being caught doing a criminal act is far more debilitating, in comparison to many transitory physical pains most of us suffer during the course of our life.

Pain has another interesting side to it. While it is on, it is the cause of the greatest misery on earth. To a person going through intense pain, nothing else matters. It is debilitating, crippling not only to the body but also to our thought process. People going through pain cannot think of anything except the pain they are going through. None of your dearest friends can possibly share that physical pain which is absolutely non-substitutable. But as soon as you are relieved of that pain, either by some treatment or by the disappearance of the cause of the pain, you wonder if anything of that kind ever happened to you. That phase of pain becomes history and goes into the deep recesses of our sub-conscious. All pains, we must understand affect the living being. The dead do not experience it, they have no memory, no sensation and hence the person dying becomes completely immune to it. Indeed, death is a great reliever and in the context of life and death phenomenon, it is always welcome. Death in fact, is the most effective and potent anesthesia any man has ever produced.

Sensation of any kind of pain is the biggest cause of any form of misery. When in pain, a person cannot think straight and is incapable of performing any of his normal functions with adequate concentration. A patient suffering from a serious affliction, when on an operation table, is worried more about the anticipated pain caused by the surgeon's knife than the serious disease that he is likely to be cured of, by that cut. The threshold of tolerance of physical pain in all living beings is extremely low. Our survival instinct also, in first instance, acts to prevent any infliction of pain and only if the perception of threat to life appears stronger, resorts to other steps to ward of the danger to life. One observes an interesting series of events at the funeral ceremony of our near and dear ones. In case of cremation, before the pyre is lit, all friends and relatives are seen touching the body very fondly, performing all the rituals with great reverence sitting close to the body. As soon as the fire is lit, everyone moves away as far as one can, to stay at safe distance. The burning body and fire has the potential to cause injury and pain to the living. The dead ones are of course, immune to it.

Excessive pain sometimes creates irrational behaviour and affects our capacity to think straight. The advent of modern science and technology has vastly improved our quality of life, indeed, has made it much more comfortable than that of our ancestors. It has also made us less tolerant of any discomfort and pain. Even in the field of medical sciences, while the main emphasis is on curing the disease, the methodology being applied is gradually becoming non-invasive causing minimal pain.

In any accident, even in those that involve serious threat to life, relief from pain is the first priority of the victim. Everything else including important life-saving treatment can wait.

Human beings, because of their heightened cognitive faculties, vis-à-vis other living beings, suffer from another syndrome. They want to live on for ever. Death marks the termination of their identity and their ego finds it difficult to reconcile to that reality. It creates anxiety and helplessness from where there is no redemption. This concern usually stems from our attachment to things material, our worldly possession which most of us have acquired painstakingly over many years. This concern is also on display for some of our friends and relations, with whom we have bonded for years and whose fate we feel is somehow linked with ours.

It is important to realize that nothing in this world which is of material nature, including human body is of permanent nature and all of them must perish when their time is ripe. Secondly, there is something in every human being, indeed in every living being which is of a permanent nature. Death therefore, does not mean a termination. It is only a form of a renewal and those who have realized it, do not exhibit any anxiety or fear. Those who wish to live for ever, which at best can only be in the memory of those left behind, are advised to perform good karmas. That alone is the legacy one can leave behind. The legacy of the dead does not consist in the wealth they have acquired, or in the position they have held, or successful career that they had for themselves. It is only in the good karmas, the service and help they have extended to others.

The Gita makes an interesting observation about such people in Chapter 6, Shloka 40:

Parth Naiveh Namutra
Vinash Tasya Vidhyate
Na Hi Kalyankrit Kaschit
Durgatim Tat Gachhti

"One, who is constantly engaged in performing good deeds and in service to others, is never destroyed either in this birth or any time thereafter".

Unfortunately, our obsession with our self and with the material wealth, does not allow us to develop any sensitivity towards our fellow beings, especially with the less fortunate ones. Nobody is suggesting complete renunciation or abdication of one's responsibility towards one's dependents, but certain amount of concern for others and for those in need does not hurt. In fact, the Gita counsels all of us to keep performing our duties with utmost devotion and perform such tasks that benefit a large number of people without expecting anything in return. Only then can we conquer death, though metaphorically. Such beings live on for ever. One look at the lives of all those who are remembered by successive generations in this world, will convince us of the veracity of this statement. They left a legacy, not of enormous material wealth, but of great deeds that created something of enormous value for the entire humanity.

Fear of the unknown is disturbing to all of us. The unknown is mysterious, an enigma that we wish to unravel but do not succeed, no matter how hard we try. It is not as if no one has tried that before, but no one has succeeded so far and no one is likely to. Science with several spectacular achievements to its credit has completely failed to solve the riddle of death and what happens thereafter. In any case, this is a subject that is not likely to find mention in any science book or any document dealing with the material world. There is no primary evidence or description of an experience after death, recounted by any living being that can be taken on record and certified for its authenticity.

This is a subject that eminently qualifies however, for a mention only in some spiritual books, if at all. There are two such spiritual treatises amongst others that deal with this matter extensively, and interestingly, both make an identical statement about, death as a phenomenon, what happens after, nature and the identity of soul and relationship of karmas with birth and death. The Bhagwad Gita, has dealt with subject in great detail when, Arjuna refuses to fight a war with his kith and kin in the battle of Mahabharata and be responsible for their death. Krishna, regarded as an incarnation of the Supreme God, painstakingly delivers his discourse running into three hundred thousand words, wherein He tries to disabuse the mind of Arjuna of great misgivings he had about death, rebirth, soul, our duties, our objective in life and scores of other subjects that concern all of us here.

Another authority that is often quoted by the pundits to deliver a sermon to a religious congregation, as is customary at ceremonies attendant on the death of an individual, is drawn from Kathoupanishad. This scripture has been derived from an ancient Hindu book called Yajurveda, one of the four oldest written documents of the Vedanta philosophy. There is an interesting conversation between Nachiketa, who has been gifted by his father to Yama, the Lord of death and Yama grants three wishes to Nachiketa, who is keen to know only the truth about death and afterlife. Yama, after great reluctance, bound as he is to the wishes granted by him, explains at length, facts about death, afterlife, soul, Supreme power and several other facets of human existence in the universe. Those desirous of a detailed description of various phenomena related to death and afterlife may refer to these documents.

We need to pause here and raise a poser. What if we get to know about the truth relating to our fate after death? Will it make fear of death disappear or any less? Will this knowledge make everyone perform only good deeds while they live? Will the world in a holistic sense, become a better place, free of evil and remain so for ever? It is difficult to hazard a guess, but initial impression is that answer to all the questions raised above would be negative. Nothing would change in this world, indeed nothing has changed over aeons and mere discovery of a few facts about life and death phenomena is not likely to change the world and the people that inhabit it. Knowledge of another life after death may motivate some people to postpone the performance of good deeds to the next life. Present life will perhaps be dedicated to the cause of complete enjoyment and in performing some evil acts that may not hurt their interests.

Krishna, in Chapter 4, Shloka 5 of the Gita tells Arjuna:

Bahuni Me Vyatitani
Janmani Tav Charjuna
Tanyam Ved Sarvani
Na Tvam Veth Parantapa

"You and I have had several births in this world. I know them all, but you have no knowledge of any of them".

In order for all of us to have several births, especially in a situation where our body is perishable, we must have an identity that is eternal and becomes a veritable carrier of several bodies in an extended phase of time and space. In other words our distinct identity that is, an entity with an ID must exist in the universal context to be able to resurface time and again. A legitimate question that arises is that how long does this go on? We shall seek the authority of the Gita to find an answer to these and related questions.

Chapter 9 of the Gita describes the entire sequence of events and the phenomena attendant on frequency of life and death. It would be worthwhile to reproduce following four shloka:

Sarvabhutani Kaunteya
Prakritim Yanti Mamikam
Kalpakshye Punastani
Kalpado Visrijamyaham *Shloka 7*

Krishna tells Arjuna, "At the end of every era that marks the end of the universe, all beings merge with My identity. I again create them at the beginning of the new era".

Prakritim Svam Ashtabhya
Vrisijami Puna Puna
Bhutgramimam Kritsnam
Vashm Prakrite Vashat *Shloka 8*

Krishna adds: "Strictly under the influence of my nature, I create and recreate the entire living organism in accordance with their karmas",

Te Tam Bhuktva Swarglokam Vishalam
Khshine Punye Martyalokam Vishanti
Aivam Trayi Dharmam Anuprapanna
Gatagatam Kamkama Labhante *Shloka 21*

"All living beings have to partake of the results of their karmas. His good karmas take him to heaven, where he reaps the benefits due to him. Those desirous of material pleasures return to the world thereafter".

Aham Hi Sarva Yagyanam
Bhokta Cha Prabhurev Cha
Na Tu Mambhi Jananti
Tatven Ata Chyavanti Te

"I am the owner and user of all karmas. Those who are ignorant of this immutable truth, remain subjected to the cycle of several births and deaths".

Yanti Devvrata Devan
Pitrin Yanti Pitrivrata
Bhutani Yanti Bhutejya
Yanti Madhyajinopi Mam

Reiterating the importance of karmas and worship, Krishna says: "All his devotees who worship Him with complete dedication attain Him and get out of the circle of life and death".

Continuous process of life and death of all living beings, is an essential attribute of nature and under its influence, God or the Supreme energy creates, destroys and then creates again in accordance with the karmas of that living being. Destruction and regeneration are an integral part of the dynamics of this universe and that is what sustains it, in the shape and state that we find it in. Just imagine a situation where there were no deaths and no new births. This world will present a pathetic picture of living beings of different vintage, suffering from all kinds of physical and mental disorders and spreading nothing but large-scale depression all around. Who would want such a world? Old, sick, boring, bereft of any energy and youthfulness, stereotyped and worst of all, a world that looks utterly hopeless and helpless.

Young, fresh and new would always remain the preferred option of everybody, including the conscious option expressed by the old. Youth is a symbol of energy, hope and strength, again the preferred option of an entity engaged in the perennial task of creating and destroying.

In many respects, it is necessary and desirable that we remain completely ignorant about our past or future births. Their knowledge would create absolute chaos in the society, as also in the lives of every individual who will spend all his life comparing the two or many more, and everyone would end up remaining utterly discontent.

In other words, while death of everyone born in this world is not only certain, it is also eminently desirable, knowledge and memories of different births are not.

CHAPTER 5

Our Tryst With Death

"Death can occur anytime. So be prepared."

The actual physical death of each one of us, takes place at an appointed time. One hopes and presumes that decision on the longevity of each living being, is based on certain criteria that are uniformly applied to the entire humanity or entire living world. Also, the entity or power that takes this decision must also be absolutely above board, and is not prone to any wrong calculations. It must also be completely un-amenable to any pressure or influence and act in a manner that is equal to all. The operating system governing this subject must also be completely immune from any virus. We have observed nature in its several avatars and thankfully, we may accuse it of ruthlessness and other traits that may affect us adversely, but we have never seen it being unjust or partial. The Supreme power, in who we believe that power is vested, is also known to the world as absolutely impartial and equal to all. In fact, He is described as 'Nirguna', an entity that does not possess any qualities and therefore, is not affected by any.

Some of us, the ignorant ones do not hesitate in putting the blame of our misfortune, on that Supreme power whenever it strikes us. This usually happens at the death of our dear ones. Death generates the ultimate fear and in the same strain causes the ultimate misery. The one closest to the dead and perhaps, the one most adversely affected, either because of emotional bonding or because of adverse material factors, is usually the loudest in his vilification of that Supreme entity.

Here is a piece of advice by Krishna to those stricken with grief:

> *Na Kasadychit Papam*
> *Na Chaiv Sukritam Vibhu*
> *Agyanen Avritam Gyanam*
> *Ten Muihanti Jantava*

> *Krishna tells Arjuna that He (Krishna), "assumes neither the good nor bad deeds of any living being. Widespread ignorance has covered the knowledge and those suffering from delusion make such unwise statements".*

The length of time, each one of us will live in this world, is a function of our karmas, as is the fact of our birth in human form. Usually, these are our past karmas that have a bearing on the time that we are likely to spend in this world. We normally determine the age of the deceased on the basis of number of years he has spent between his birth and death. We do this computation because that is convenient to all of us and we understand this measure correctly. However, the length of time each one of us will spend on this earth is decided by the number of breaths earmarked for this purpose. All of us have a fixed number of breaths allowed to each one of us for a lifetime. On an average, a normal adult takes about 15-16 breaths in a minute. Evidently, it is possible to increase or decrease the longevity by manipulating your breath rate. It would be stating the obvious, if we were to say that by reducing the number of breaths per minute in any given situation, it is possible to increase the time one can spend in this world. Suppose with our conscious efforts, which must become a permanent feature with the manner in which we breathe, we bring down our breath rate from 16 per minute to 12, we will effectively increase our age by a quarter. Interestingly, that is what most of the Yogis do. Those who have perfected the art of Pranayam and of regulating the time required to complete one breath, can effectively elongate their existence on earth. There are stories of several Yogis and Rishis who have stretched their period of stay in the world, a little longer than the usual, purely on the strength of their skills in regulating their breath. On the other hand, millions of us, because of ignorance of this phenomenon, shorten our lives by our intemperate behaviour, unnecessary exhibition of anger and other negative traits, leading to shorter breaths and a faster depletion of our respiratory credit balance.

A basic point of distinction between the living and dead is the capacity of the former to breathe in and breathe out, and its absence in the latter. The critical factor therefore, is the breath, its quality, our capacity at regulating it and our conscious awareness of it. It would be interesting to look at this phenomenon and the importance given by us to this activity that is fundamental to our existence.

Let us first look at the nature's benevolence in making available to us, the most valuable of our necessities in the most facile and easiest of ways. Breathing comes to us in such abundance and in such an effortless way that more often than not, we are not even aware of it. We inspire and expire in an automation mode. The fact of its extreme facility would be evident from the fact that this process goes on, even in our state of deep sleep when we are otherwise lost to the world, and are lying in a state of complete inertness. Our respiratory system keeps working, drawing in enough oxygen to make sure that our sleep does not assume a permanent nature. Adequate quantity of oxygen keeps flowing to all our vital organs even though we are not batting an eyelid.

Our profound salutations to the designer and craftsman of the human body at conceiving and crafting such a marvelous creation!

The inexhaustible supply of oxygen and its easy availability has created a situation where we take the entire breathing process for granted. Its effortless occurrence makes us completely unaware of it and most ironically, we end up paying least attention to the most essential activity of our existence. We are completely unaware of the quality of air that we breathe in and the time gap between two breaths, leave alone paying any specific attention to them. It is no surprise therefore, that the respiratory problems which also affect the function of our heart today are one of the most deadly diseases people suffer from. Healthy breathing is our lifeline, indeed our life and deserves much greater attention than what we ordinarily give.

Breathing is a phenomenon that literally stands between life and death and can teach us a few home truths about death. Our body is just a nice earthen toy, beautifully crafted that additionally has the capacity to inspire and expire. Its date of expiry however, is uncertain but would largely depend upon the way it is handled, except in certain situations where it is congenitally defective. It is also governed by all the trappings of a merchandize including the 'best before' tag. Breathing can help us understand the phenomenon of life and death in a weird practical way through the process of Pranayam.

One of the standard practices followed by the practitioners

of Yoga is described as Alom-Vilom, wherein alternatively, one nostril is used for inspiring and after holding one's breath (closing both nostrils and the mouth), for a certain specified period, it is released or expired through the other. The other nostril is used thereafter and the same procedure is followed. For our exercise, it is the holding part between the inspiration and expiration that is relevant. The time for which a person can hold his breath would depend upon the general condition of a person including, the strength of his lungs and other respiratory faculties. Try holding it for as long as you can, and you will have a near death experience. Of course, your instinct for survival will make you let go your hand pretty quickly and in any case, just in time. Death would seem somewhat like this and not very substantially different from this experience. The last breath taken by an individual, signals the event of death. The difference between the dead and living really is the ability of one to breathe, and a complete disability of another to do so. Those who wish to get over the fear of death may try this procedure. A word of caution however, must be mentioned. *Do not trust anyone else with the holding duties, not even best of your friends and in no case, your wife or mother-in-law.* Yogis, who perform this exercise regularly, largely get over the fear of death. A word of caution is in order. This exercise is essentially demonstrative in nature and does not necessarily ensure absolute disappearance of fear of death. Traditional wisdom says that something that is completely unknown generates much greater degree of fear. If there is a partial knowledge or an experience of that phenomenon, the fear factor would be substantially reduced.

Important point however, that needs to be underlined is that we must consciously attempt to comprehend death and several myths that are associated with it, all of which strike terror in our weak hearts. Cowards, and majority of us belong to that class, die many times more than actual physical death which obviously takes place only once in a lifetime.

Unfortunately, our attachment to the living body creates all the confusion and delusion. This starts very early in life. A newly born child gets all the attention from his parents, brothers, sisters and other relatives, who spoil him with their love and attention. He remains perpetually attached to one or the other and learns the art and necessity of attachment. Any kind of attachment must mean love, warmth and all things pleasant. This goes into his subconscious and is impossible to be replaced by any lesser emotion. This attachment through the bodies of his family gets a further boost as he steps into the world, where again many pleasant experiences and attractions, tighten the grip of attachment. Conversely, prospects of detachment from a body create fear, and actual detachment brings in sorrow and misery. Interestingly, various events that take place in our life and those that leave an impact, encourage a sense of attachment. Very few events teach us sanguinity or spirit of renunciation. We also know that everything that is material will perish when its time comes, and its inevitable separation will cause agony and misery.

Viewed from this perspective, one is forced to look at life as something that is not a great cause of celebration. *In a certain way, our existence on the planet is one long sentence, literally, physically and metaphorically and death is only a punctuation after which the sentence continues till there is a full stop.* A complete cessation in the cycle of birth and death will happen only when we have realized the truth. This may never happen and if it does, it may take several births in human form, continuously performing good deeds and with a complete surrender to the Supreme energy.

Viewed from a higher perspective, the cycle of life and death presents a great paradox. Birth that marks a renewal is welcomed as a happy event and for the immediate family members, means great joy in terms of continuing with their lineage and identity. This also operates as a cause of grief and misery as and when it converts into death. In other words, both events are harbingers of joy and sorrow and part of the duality that one observes in all areas of universal applications. This dual nature of all subjects in this universe creates a corresponding impact on the pattern of behaviour that we exhibit all our life. We are full of immense joy one moment and down in the dumps with intense grief, the next. All our life, we remain caught in the extremes, oscillating like the pendulum of a clock and refuse to seek any sense of equanimity in our conduct. This phenomenon plays havoc with our body and intellect. Events connected with life and death, cause these opposing states and affect us in their extremes, with all other lesser emotions thrown in at different phases of our life.

The Gita advises restraint and stability in our thoughts and behaviour in all matters and events that affect us either directly or remotely. The two shlokas below are worth following:

Sukh Dukhe Same Kritva
Labhalabho Jayajayo
Tato Yudhaye Yujasya
Naivam Papam Vapsyasi *Chapter 2, Shloka 38*

"Treat joy and happiness, loss and profit, victory and defeat on an equal footing. Fight the battles of your life and you will never come to any harm".

Yogasth Kuru Karmani
Sangam Tyaktva Dhananjye
Sidhyasidhyo Samo Bhutva
Samatvam Yog Uchayate *Chapter 2, Shloka 48*

"A person installed in yoga, performs all his assigned duties with complete detachment. He remains unaffected by the consequences of his actions. That is described as 'Samatva Bhav'."

Samatva bhav in all our transactions will ensure peace and tranquility and make us remain completely sanguine. Events of life and death will also create a similar attitude like any other transaction that takes place in the ordinary course. We would learn to take everything in our stride and remain engaged in our work with complete dedication. This is the greatest mantra of success that not only creates value proposition in your job, but also sets an example for others in their pursuit of success and excellence. If you hold a position of eminence in society and wish to continue to do so on a long run, your conduct has to be exemplary and cannot possibly exhibit weakness of any kind. This weakness is also exhibited in the form of weak heart that shows emotional fragility and breaks down at any loss of a personal nature. Death of a family member or of near and dear one is one such occasion, where our inner strength and conduct is tested and closely observed by others.

In fact, this is one occasion when, not only our courage and forbearance are tested we often exhibit a behaviour that smacks of utter selfishness and pretentiousness. Sometimes, the entire scene which is meant to be marked with solemnity becomes comical. Some of the survivors of a family where death has taken place indulge in a behaviour that is absolutely contrary to the spirit of the occasion, showing uncontrollable grief is one of them. Crying and screaming appears completely unbecoming. A rational analysis of the events that unfold themselves at such occasions would reveal the utter futility of such conduct and behaviour.

According to the law of average, death usually takes place at a ripe age. The deceased person has lived his life fully and gracefully and perhaps left a legacy which may also consist of some material significance. His death, for his survivors signifies separation from the body of that person, which from the deceased point of view has become decrepit and incapable of carrying on with his normal functions. Seen from his perspective and his condition, death is a welcome event which also marks the end of his miseries and those attending on him. Logically speaking, when one becomes an encumbrance rather than an aid, it is really the best time to go. In any case, any exhibition of sorrow or grief will not affect or reach the deceased.

Now for those left behind, it is equally important to understand that the news of their grief is not likely to reach or affect the deceased. Who then are they grieving for? The other probable reason for their conduct perhaps is their unrequited love for the dead and separation from him causes unbearable pain. Another reason could be that they wish to tell the world how close they were to him and his death is a great irreparable loss. There could even be some hidden agenda behind it. The deceased in certain cases is the main provider for some people and his death marks the end of material support. The deprived ones express their grief on the loss of that support.

Even a superficial analysis of all these reasons will tell us about the futility, indeed the immorality of such behaviour. Most people exhibit such unseemly behaviour out of reasons that are entirely personal and selfish. Our society has also unnecessarily romanticized death as huge event that must be accompanied with some sound and fury. In fact, if those close to the deceased do not cry or appear drowned in inconsolable misery, they are dubbed as freaks. Others expect and wait for those affected to look miserable. In real terms, all this is occasioned by a phenomenon called attachment which really is at the root of all our miseries in life and death.

Death of an individual at a ripe age is in fact a 'cause celebre'. In some communities, the funeral procession of an elderly person is accompanied with great pomp and show and sometimes resembles a wedding procession. And there is a logic behind it which indicates new birth, a renewal and regeneration. It is important to understand that these are not the fictional fantasies of people struck by sorrow or working under hallucinatory influences, but of those who firmly believe in the continuation of life after death, existence of a permanent entity called soul and ultimate merger with the Supreme entity that controls this universe.

Having described the events that are seen at the death that takes place in a natural way, there are people dying prematurely and in circumstances that are indeed painful and unnatural. We need to adopt a sanguine stance at such occasions. One ordinarily expects everyone born to live for a reasonable length of time and indeed, for an average life span of human beings. However, nature and natural forces do not function according to the mathematical or statistical averages and here, influence of everyone's karmas plays the pivotal role. It is also not possible to create any distributive mechanism like in the case of material wealth, where a young person could take away some years from the lives of very old people, with a promise to return it in the next birth.

It is however interesting to see doctor's view in general and reaction to death of his own patient in particular. To him, death of a patient is no more than what losing a case, is to a lawyer. He has to try as hard as he can, to save the lives of several patients that he attends to, but beyond a point he does become helpless. Perhaps in that respect his helplessness is stronger than that of a lawyer because he is fighting against forces that are far more powerful. He is only armed with science and prayer, and cannot possibly have any control over supernatural forces that play an important role in a life and death situation.

An undertaker, a man at the cremation ground and the doctor are people who get to witness largest number of deaths during their lifetime. A first few occurrences perhaps shake them a little but overtime, all incidents of death, except that of their own kith and kin, cause very little emotional changes in them. They learn to, and perhaps have to take all such incidents in their stride.

Interestingly, contrary to our perception those who die prematurely or under circumstances that we would describe as painful are not necessarily unfortunate ones. Some of them may even be the blessed ones whose term as living beings in this world has come to an end. They would have lived through the effect of their karmas and are fit to attain reunion with the ultimate. The life and death of Jesus Christ should be enough to convince anyone of the veracity of this statement. The end of Krishna was also occasioned by a painful wound caused by a poisonous arrow. These personages had obliterated the impact of their negative karmas, if any, by their last act of intense sufferance.

There is a common perception that the death of some noble persons, heralds the ultimate end and release from the bondage of life-death cycle. Some of them also undergo an acute suffering before they die. Explanation of this phenomenon also lies in the principles of karmic theory. Those noble souls, who are eminently ready for their final merger with the ultimate reality, must live out their residual negative karmas before joining Him. He the Supreme power, would not accept anybody in his fold unless that somebody has washed out all the effects of his karmas, and assumed a status which is as pure as that of the Supreme reality. It would be relevant to quote the example of a great soul known as Swami Ramkrishna Paramhansa, who suffered on account of throat cancer during the last few years of his corporeal existence. The entire world believes, and not without reasons that he has attained the ultimate nirvana.

Science and spirituality has complete convergence on the question of effects of all actions. In other words, nothing in this universe is ever wasted and all our karmas create an impact and give some result. All sciences, including social, physical and biological confirm the cause and effect phenomena and their universal acceptability. The same is true of all our karmas which in consequence of our imperfect nature must necessarily comprise different shades of good and bad. Both will create an impact and give corresponding results. The effect of both kinds of karmas, have to be inevitably accepted only by us and none other. This must therefore, largely explain the variations, difference in our life pattern, longevity and the events that will affect each one of us, strictly in accordance with our actions.

Notwithstanding, every soul must get redemption in the fullness of time. But the fact is, for that to happen it is dependent on the living beings and their karmas, which again in the fullness of time must mature leading to soul's release. This of course happens, but the pace and number is woefully slow.

Chapter 6

Death in Public Domain

"Those who live for others, never die."

Death affects all and sundry except the person who is dead. The dead is gone, gone beyond any sense of pain and misery. There is not a single living person on this planet that has not been affected by it. There is this famous story of a woman who lost her only child and came running to Buddha, crying and wailing uncontrollably. She placed her dead child at Buddha's feet and pleaded with him to infuse life back into him. Buddha was very patient and asked her to calm down. He then asked her to leave her child with him and go back to the town where she lived. The woman raised the pitch of her wailing a few notches higher and requested Buddha to do something or else she would kill herself. She apparently did not wish to live after her only child is gone. Buddha whereupon told her to go back to her place with a specific purpose, which was to enquire from as many households as she could visit, whether there has been a death in their family. In fact, in a more dramatic move, he asked her to get sesame seeds from that household which had not seen death.

Evidently, no household in the entire town offered seeds to her. She returned empty handed and fell at Buddha's feet. This time her emotions in paying obeisance to Buddha were entirely different.

Some thing that happens to everybody and happens all the time becomes a non-event. It no longer falls in the public domain. It is something like the energy which is everywhere and hence no where, that is, it cannot be seen at one place. Death takes place everywhere and to everyone and hence does not affect the world at large. In any case, it is not a subject matter of public debate or discussion unless it happens in an unusual manner. Even then there is no novelty because over the years, apart from natural deaths, there are many that are occasioned under unusual circumstances. Reinforced with this logic again death should not be an occasion for uncontrolled misery over an extended period. Indeed, it deserves to be treated like any other event that occurs and passes by.

Death ordinarily, is not a subject matter of public debate. It happens only to one person but seems to ostensibly affect everyone except the person who is dead. The dead person is beyond any discussion or any other issue connected with his death. He does not become part of the possible causes of death, the legacy left behind by him, the manner of the disposal of his mortal remains (unless spoken to somebody during his lifetime or leaving a written note), contents and the interpretation of the language of his will, if any. Only the living contributes to the discussion that affects him and he does not indeed, cannot have any say in the matter that concerns him.

All this however, remains within the four corners of the household and a few relatives who profess to be close to him or the family. They are the ones who take decisions with respect to his mortal remains. It is therefore important that they remain in a state of sound mind and not get affected with grief that prevents them from taking the right decision, however small or insignificant.

These are same set of people that are most closely affected by the death of the individual. Ordinarily, they are also the ones who are deeply grief-stricken. Ironically, they are also the ones who would push the body of their dearest one, out of the house at the earliest. The reason for their uncontrolled grief may be emotional, but in reality their overt action in sending the body out are purely physical and practical. Any suggestion to keep the body in the house would be met by strong disapproval by those very people who loved the deceased dearly, and who looked utterly miserable at his death.

None of the close friends and relatives in their sound mind would offer to place their dead friend's body in their home even for a second. In some societies, the reasons for refusal are both practical as well as superstitious. Any attempt by the affected household to keep the body longer than what is absolutely essential, would be met with huge protests by the neighbours and would be socially frowned upon. The reasons are entirely practical in nature and override the strongest possible emotional upsurge evidenced by members of the family. Once the rigor mortis sets in, the body starts decomposing into the elements and the organic waste, and no living being is ever known to be comfortable with the elements in their raw form or with the organic waste. This is elementary. Human bodies and the bodies of all living beings are designed to remain in a healthy state only when they are living. They rot and stink when they are dead. They are only a shade better than the garbage that all housewives throw away willingly. They must go back to the elementary stage to be built up again for another body.

The mortal remains of all living entities must merge with the elements of nature for a process of renewal. The new bodies verily have to be reconstructed from the organic material that is present in the universe and has to be recycled for creating a continuum. The construction material for all the new bodies that inevitably have to be created by the master have to be procured from here and is not imported from any other planet. This is also an integral part of the cosmic energy that must remain constant in its aggregate form but keeps manifesting itself in a variety of ways, including the births and deaths of various living entities.

Interestingly, all of us in that respect are interconnected. The concept of cosmic energy binds us together and different life species are created out of the common pool of this vast energy reservoir, live our lives again in accordance with the quality and quantity of energy contributed by us to the common pool. This is where the importance and relevance of our karmas comes in. With the same logic, all of us are equal to start with, and difference in our forms and substance are caused by our own karmas during long series of deaths and births. Destruction, renewal, degeneration and regeneration must inevitably, take place all around.

This is how all of us become part of the public domain, and a small but significant part of the universal and ubiquitous energy. We are all identical, and equal. Proper understanding of this phenomenon will create a beautiful spread effect, effectively diluting any sense of grief we may experience on the death of any individual. This knowledge must also clear any misgivings about our relationships with our fellow beings across the planet, and remove all prejudices that we carry with us all our lives on the basis of colour, caste, creed, or gender. An enlightened awareness of this fact, though rare, will also create this world more healthy and peaceful to live in.

All of us are like a drop of water in an ocean. The ocean is vast and is made up of trillions and trillions of drops. All that the ocean contains is water that appears to be of different colour at different places around the globe. It is warm here and cold there. Somewhere the quantity is huge and it is very deep. At some other location it would be shallow. It is largely calm and quiet, but there are times and places where it assumes a very aggressive stance. Moon's gravitation pull causes huge tidal waves and sometimes, make the ocean behave in a weird fashion and can cause massive destruction. Ocean has its varied moods and a keen student of oceanography will be in a position to present a graphic description of the ocean in its muliticoloured and multifaceted avatar.

Does it not sound familiar? Eventually, these are the tiny drops of water that create an ocean that behaves like it does in different ways. Human being like the drops of water indeed, behave exactly the same way as the ocean in its aggregate and sometimes in a disaggregate form. Usually the calm surface of the ocean belies what keeps happening down under. No body ever knows what goes on inside the breast of a man. One moment it is calm and the next it may become a volcano of emotions that might erupt any time, a condition one often observes at the time of death.

Death of all living beings, as a general rule falls outside the public domain. It is very much a personalized event, and all the rest except the dead are affected only marginally depending upon their relationship and attachment with the dead. The degree of the impact on others would also depend on their attachment and dependence on the dead in the material context. To the world at large it is a non-event and at best, is treated like any other news one reads in the newspaper. The extent of sorrow, sympathy and other emotions exhibited by others are also more a function of their normal nature, and really have little to do with the dead.

Much of the emotional and physical stress following the death of a person has to be borne by the immediate members of the family. That is really stating the obvious. The physical part lasts only a day or two but it is the emotional aspect that lingers on for a longer period of time, and here again the fact of attachment and dependence becomes relevant. For any grief or physical hurt, time they say is the biggest healer. No truer words were ever said. Interestingly, everybody's own life must go on and there are so many occupations in one's own daily routine that it is improbable, indeed impossible for him, however close he may have been to the deceased, to sit back and grieve over his loss. It is impractical and perhaps, would happen only in the case of the rarest of the rare. Even on the ceremonial front, you may bring in flowers and place them on the mantelpiece where the memories of the deceased lie in the form of a photograph, for a few days. This activity will also peter into a routine chore and fresh flowers would, before long be replaced by the artificial ones. You cannot keep on serving the cause of the dead beyond an acceptable level. Such are the pressures of one's own life that the demands and the exigencies of the dead, become obsolete and are easily dispensed with. Beyond a certain period, all things connected with the dead become irrelevant without becoming irreverent though, and he remains just a memory without any associated physical evidence.

Extended grief and indeed, frequent reference to the dead as an example of good behaviour and his comparison to those who are living also becomes a taboo sometimes. It may be all right to remember those gone by with fond memories, but their comparison with those who are living is often met with strong disapproval, especially by those that are compared against. A repeated reference often meets with strong disapproval even from those not affected. Usually it is customary not to talk ill of the dead, even though he may have been a rascal all his life.

We all tend to become a little charitable towards the dead, either because we expect no further harm from him or because of our own similar fate few years down the line.

It is interesting how human nature suddenly changes its view of a person on his death. In a study, photographs of three people unknown to a selected group of psychology students were shown with different expressions on their faces. They were asked to evaluate their traits in several categories, the primary one relating to morality, industriousness and other issues of social behaviour. While students were given one week to present their analysis, they were sent another communication immediately after that period. They were informed that one of the persons has died in the meanwhile, and students may take another week to report their analysis. At the end of two weeks, they were asked to send both reports, if there were two, one made at the end of the first week and another one at the end of second one.

The observations made a very interesting reading and a contrast. *The dead man suddenly became morally far superior to the other two and indeed, became a better human being in the second week's report.* The surest way one can change one's perception from a devil to a decent man is to allow death to intervene. Some of your enemies may turn out as friends, or at least shed their animosity, as soon as rigor mortis sets in.

Having described death as an exclusive phenomenon affecting the immediate family, we need to pause and reflect on certain deaths that inevitably fall within the ambit of public domain. There is a majority who lives for themselves or for their immediate family and there is a small number that lives and indeed, dies for a public cause. Living for a public cause, dying for it and both living and dying for that cause, happens only to a select few. They are the blessed ones. We have identified three species as follows:

1. There are some people who spend all or most of their life in the service of others. Their life is worthy of emulation, but in real sense they seldom attract many followers. In other words, their number usually is few and far between. Their life however, is a demonstration of absolute selflessness and they have very few needs of their own. Some of them are normal householders, but their immediate family has as much claim on their time and resources as any body else. They belong to the whole world and become an icon and a legend in their own lifetime. There are others of the same class who work tirelessly in the service of humanity but assiduously shun any public recognition. Indeed, people of this nature come into this world, do their work selflessly and go away unpublicized and unnoticed. They are anonymous workers and are justifiably placed at the highest level of humanity. Their only raison de'tre is service for others.

Swami Vivekananda, in one of his famous speeches to a western audience once, remarked that there are hundreds of Yogis like Jesus Christ and Buddha that come into this world, perform great service to the humanity at large, seek no name or favours and go away unknown. Most of us never get to know of them and their work. In most cases, they consciously stay away from the public space and keep doing their work quietly. It was a bold statement to make and indeed, a true one. It also fits into the classic concept of the aggregate cosmic energy, which usually remains in deficit on account of its heavy and continuous drawl by us, the lesser mortals. Energy balance is maintained only by the acts of such exalted souls that take away nothing and only contribute to the much required positive component. They do not add even an ounce of the negative energy. They are truly the enlightened souls and perhaps by such acts they break away permanently from the bond of birth and death, and merge with the Supreme force, their ultimate destination. The Gita in Chapter 12, Shlokas 3 and 4 says the following:

Ye Tvaksharam Anirdeshyam
Avyaktam Parupaste
Sarvatrgam Achintyam Cha
Kutastham Chalam Dhruvam

Samniyamya Indriyagramam
Sarvatra Sambhudaya
Te Prapnuvanti Mamev
Sarva Bhut Hite Rata

"Those, who have kept their senses in full control and meditate constantly on the eternal Brahma who is beyond the reach of mind and intellect, defying any description in the material context, is present everywhere, is unchanged, has no attribute and remain constantly engaged in the service of others by treating everyone as equal, doubtlessly attain Me".

One often wonders whether Krishna is talking about real people or the fictional ones, but when you look at the lives of Jesus or Buddha, or in recent times at the life and times of Mother Teresa, your surprise and disbelief turns into reality. Such personages are pure souls that have a covering of a body so that they can work amongst people that look like them without being misunderstood. They are saints and cease to remain in the human form after they leave their corporeal appearance. Although they set an example for others, there are only a few, in fact very few, that can emulate them.

However, the Gita talks about such person with great respect and says the following in Chapter 3, Shloka 21:

Yatyat Acharti Shreshtra
Tattat Devetro Jana
Sa Yat Pramanam Kurute
Loka Tat Anuvartate

"Common folks tend to follow the enlightened ones in performance of various tasks. Whatever examples are set by them, become the benchmarks".

Those who work with absolutely unselfish motive and constantly look for opportunities to serve others, become a role model. In normal conversations, their name figures in as an example worth following. Usually, parents unable to follow their examples, cite them for the benefit of their children. Interestingly, many such personages acquire a fan following during their own lifetime. In India, of course because of widespread spiritual influence, the number of such persons is quiet large, and those who work for social causes in addition to being a renowned religious figure, draw a bigger fan following. There are others who work for social cause without professing to be spiritual Guru. This country, and for that matter the world comes across very few people in the political field who can command following of such dimensions.

The last such personage that the world saw was Mahatma Gandhi. He was a tall political leader, but the kind of politics that he practised and professed was immersed in ethics and morality and that, more than anything else got him the name, the epithet Mahatma and fame with universal acceptability.

Once they leave their physical body, the entire world cries, sheds tears and pays a moving homage to them. People who join in this movement are people who cut across the boundaries of religion, caste, creed, colour and gender. Indeed gods from heaven descend to earth to pay their homage to the departed soul.

Death of such people lies entirely in the public domain.

There is a famous couplet in Hindi that runs as follows:

Jab Tum Aaye Jagat Me
Jag Hansa Tum Roye
Aise Karni Kar Chalo
Tum Hanso Jag Roye

"When you came into the world, you cried and the world laughed. Live your life in such a way and perform such acts that after you are gone, the world weeps and you laugh".

2. Then there are those who die for a public cause. The obvious reference is to the uniformed personnel. Army, Air force, Navy, paramilitary forces in every country, deploy personnel for routine protection of its national assets including its citizenry and the police constabulary for the maintenance of law and order and other sundry duties.

   The military that every country must deploy for guarding its frontiers renders great service for the nation. It is charged with the responsibility of protecting and preserving its honour and sovereignty and ordinarily discharges it with great élan and commitment. Their service is of perennial nature, acting as sentinels during peacetime and as fighters during a war that is either initiated by them or is thrust upon them. They are a highly disciplined force and do not exercise any independent will in the event of an actual or a perceived threat or emergency. While the Army guards the nation on the ground level, the Air force guards the air space as well as provides air cover in the event of a war. Navy of course, is charged with the task of protecting the extended and notional water front usually with respect to the sea or seas that besiege a country.

The nature of duties, even those in the province of routine are arduous and call for great grit, stamina and determination not required in the field of duties that others perform in the service of the nation. The politicians, civil service and engineers and host of other personnel engaged in the service of the country ostensibly, are never subjected to the rigours and challenges that the military is required to perform even during peacetime. It is therefore not without reason that their services are accorded the highest recognition amongst the hierarchies of services that any citizen of the nation is called upon to perform. The risk involved, are also much higher than by anybody in the civilian space.

Apart from guarding the frontiers of the country in utterly inhospitable conditions and away from the comforts and warmth of their families, the military personnel are also called upon to quell serious disturbances in the social and civilian fronts. Many are known to have lost their lives during non-war situations as well. Unnatural events like floods, earthquakes and other natural calamities are also some of the occasions when these personnel have rendered phenomenal service to protect life and property. These are all dangerous and risky ventures where many a soldiers have lost their precious lives.

Without being judgmental about the normal work and nature of these people, indeed, most of them are common people with no claim to extraordinary powers or fame they lay down their lives in the service of others. They die so that others can live in peace. They ask no questions when called upon to perform.

Such personnel are also in the public domain and their death too lies there. They are of course, grieved over by their family, but the entire nation grieves and salutes them and their sacrifice. Depending on the nature of their sacrifice, majority of them are immortalized and the nation shows its gratitude to these brave hearts by inscribing their names and memory in stone and other memorials. They are also remembered by the nation collectively on the occasion of certain designated national events.

3. Mention must be made of a large number of other people who render great service in a routine manner, through the instrumentality of their normal work and assigned duties. They perform these tasks as Karamyogis. They remain completely detached from the work and its rewards. Indeed, the rewards that flow from their tireless pursuits are also dedicated to the public cause and impact their lives in a variety of positive ways. Scientists, statesmen, social activists, musicians, artists, painters of world renown and several other public figures who have stepped out of their personal space and have done something extraordinary for others, must necessarily come within public domain. They are all ordinary people, unrecognizable in a crowd and lead an ordinary existence like all the rest of us. But they have one uncommon trait. They have fire of ambition burning in their breast to do

something extraordinary for the benefit of mankind. They have dedication, perseverance and a single minded devotion to the cause that they pursue.

Usually, that cause lies primarily in one field in which they seek excellence. They are people who are not necessarily successful by the standard yardstick of success in terms of power and wealth, though that is not a taboo for any of them. But their main concern is to achieve something of substance by which others can benefit and benefit for a long time. Rabindranath Tagore, Sir C.V. Raman, Visveswarya, Sir Homi Bhaba are some of the people in that class. They become legends in their lifetime. They do not sacrifice their lives for any cause, but pursue a cause during their life to create enormous value and benefit for others. They are veritable torch bearers and demonstrate for others what can possibly be achieved by intellectual and physical perseverance, against all odds. They do possess a spiritual streak, but their spirituality assumes a different shade and consists essentially of worship through work. They are true Karamyogis with or without the tag of spirituality attached to their work. They seek actualization not necessarily through the traditional means of devotion, but see that in their own work and achieve it through work alone.

Their kind of yoga has been beautifully described in Shloka 50 of Chapter 2 of Bhagwad Gita in following words:

Budhiyukto Jahatih Ha
Ubhe Sukrit Dushkrite
Tasmat Yogaye Yujaysva
Yoga Karmasu Kaushlam

> *"Yogi with stable intellect gives up his sins and virtues in this world and is freed from their bondage. To him yoga really means achieving excellence in the field of his own work".*

The incident of their death, natural or accidental also lies in the public domain. Their physical presence ceases to become an issue and they verily live through their work. Whenever their work or the product is made use of, their name is mentioned with respect and admiration.

We have another set of very ordinary people from amongst the masses, who generally lead a very mundane existence. They ordinarily, do nothing spectacular and are never mentioned in dispatches, either for great act of goodness or for extreme evil behaviour. They are nice decent people living next door who want to discharge their responsibility to the best of their ability. They do not hurt anybody, nor are they famous or known outside their limited circle of friends and relatives. They constitute a class that is commonly referred to as common people.

Interestingly, there comes a time and indeed an opportunity in the life of everybody including, in the lives of the common people we talked about, when they are challenged to do something extraordinary. Sometime these opportunities are thrust upon them. It could be an act that calls for grit and courage, like risking one's own life to save another, or protecting the modesty of some unknown person without expecting any reward or anything in return. There are no pre-determined occasions for an exhibition of bravery by such common people, who do not wish to become a hero or a celebrity, but circumstances perhaps leave no options for them but to act. If they end up saving a life or two at the cost of their own life, their death becomes part of the public domain. These acts are performed on the spur of the moment and the decision to risk one's life to protect or save another is also taken instantaneously.

Our world is often subjected to major natural calamities resulting in death and destruction of great magnitude. Several lives are lost and many can be saved by human intervention that requires courage of the highest order. Those who save the lives of others by endangering their own are also honoured either in their life or in a posthumous way.

The animal and human world has many things in common and one of them is the strong survival instinct. Animals largely, live for themselves because that is part of their intrinsic nature. Most human beings also live for themselves, but there are some who on the basis of certain values and convictions, or on account of opportunities that come their way, demonstrate their willingness to live and die for others. Only such people live for ever and others only exist, and that also only for the period that their physical being permits them to.

It would be interesting to observe that only such deaths that occur in pursuance of a public cause, or in defense of one's motherland, or in fighting injustice, become public events. Death of a tall and well known public figure, rendering selfless service during his lifetime and respected by every one, also falls in the public domain. All other deaths are non-events.

It is true that the deaths that belong to public domain, affect much larger number of people than those that affect a family or few friends. However, even in these cases, the public memory is short and the importance and relevance of such events also die gradually. Human mind and intellect are designed in such a way that they show distinct preference for happy and cheerful happenings. We possess weakness and are, partial to things that are positive and agreeable and consciously avoid those that are unpleasant and distasteful. That has been the general tendency all throughout and the reasons are not difficult to understand. We have therefore evolved overtime to fondly remember the agreeable and reject the disagreeable.

Human memory is extremely short for deaths of any kind and the public memory on a collective basis is shorter. It is inadvisable hence to become a martyr or pretend to become one in our daily routine. It definitely does not pay if one tries to become one, without any worthy cause. Also, grief over the death of near and dear ones, for an unusually extended period ceases to draw any sympathy from the expected quarters. On the contrary, beyond a point it may meet with strong disapproval from those very people who in the normal course, are expected to sympathize and console. Death is a universal and an essential phenomenon, and its universality takes away any novelty that may be experienced by those who may have encountered it for the first time, or of some one that was important to them.

One can draw a beautiful analogy from a fundamental and universal truth based on a scientific reality. Some thing that is supposed to be everywhere is not seen at one place or cannot be seen anywhere. One of the attributes of God is His omnipresence and hence He is seen nowhere. Closer to ground reality, the sky and air are supposed to be everywhere and not seen anywhere. Death that takes place everywhere and all the time, on the same analogy is a non-event.

Mention must also be made in passing, of certain deaths that are as painful as they are a blot on the name of the society.

These relate to the deaths of unwanted newly born that are abandoned by their mothers for fear of public condemnation. You find these little souls in garbage bins, outside a hospital or on the door steps of an orphanage. These deaths though, in a public domain are not remembered and indeed are forgotten as fast as they are abandoned by the unwilling mothers. Death, which also means an end to life, is equally reprehensible, when caused by millions of abortions that take place around the world. Millions of criminals and pleasure seekers of the world, only bring collective shame to the civilized society by shirking from the responsibility of their brazen acts.

Chapter 7

Death—The Great Leveler

"The dead can do no wrong. Long live the dead."

Death washes away all the sins and grants the ultimate pardon even to the most evil and vicious of the human beings. Even the most obdurate amongst us, would show remarkable willingness to relent and forgive the dead, all his misdemeanors committed during his lifetime. In that respect, it is something eminently desirable from the point of view of the dead and the living, and the sinner and sinned against. But this is just a short term view of our existence in this universe and might just please only those who subscribe to the concept of one birth and one death. This class of non believers would refuse to accept the existence of an entity called Soul, which is deemed eternal and indestructible. That other view, places soul beyond the reach of death and believes it to be of a permanent nature and an integral part of that Supreme energy known as God. This is a subject that requires separate attention and a comprehensive delineation. However at this stage, it must be said that the specific cause of enmity between the two individuals is normally obliterated by the death of one of them.

Unfortunately, this world is full of some very weird people who would seek to carry out their vendetta against the survivors and heirs of the deceased. But thankfully, that is more of an exception than a rule.

In some manner, death seems to purge the dead, of all his sins. Since there is no greater punishment for a person than the termination of his existence from the world, those wronged by the living appear to adopt a charitable view on the death of the accused. Interestingly, in every society the survivors of the person killed or murdered do not rest till they succeed in bringing the culprit to justice. The ultimate justice for them really means sending that person to the gallows. They seem to believe that the wronged person's soul will rest in peace only when a similar treatment has been meted out to the criminal. In every civilized society, it is important to make a distinction between administration of justice or enforcement of law on one hand, and wreaking vengeance and infliction of similar punishment on the person who has allegedly caused injury.

The lord of death is not known to make any distinction between the rich and poor, strong and weak, prince and pauper or high and low. The mightiest of the world also succumb to it at the appointed time. The megalomaniacs of the world, and we see many of them in different phases of history arrogate to them unlimited powers, including the power to play God. Their end is also as certain as that of a man with no ambition. On the other side of the spectrum, all men of God, including the God himself living a life in a human form, must face death like an ordinary mortal. All good things and the worst of evil persona must perish in the fullness of time.

Time indeed, has a strong correlation with the phenomena of death in a variety of ways. The time of death, time a person has spent on this earth, (his age) time after his death, time to bring down the intensity of grief of those affected by it, are all factors that have a significant bearing on the event of death. Time, they say is a great healer. It is also a great leveler.

It is essential to fully comprehend the anatomy of life-death cycle, not merely from the point of reconciling with it, but also accept it as a fact of our existence. We must know and understand that nothing in this universe is for ever. In fact, as a broad generalization, everything that is visible will perish. The shelf life of different objects may vary, but perish they all will. This is absolutely true of all gross objects. For the subtle however, there are a few exceptions. Firstly, all subtle entities which are beyond the influence of the natural elements never die. The Soul for instance, is permanent, eternal and being an integral part of the supreme energy, remains in the universe for ever. It does not change one bit. There are other subtle phenomena like the thoughts, speech, intellect and ego which also do not die and remain somewhere in the universe in the form of imperishable energy. But unlike the soul, these not being an integral part of the supreme energy, change their forms and become indistinguishable. While the soul is pure and pristine and does not affect anybody, either in this birth or hereinafter, other subtle entities enumerated above must necessarily cause an effect. They manifest themselves in different forms which really is a phenomenon that is beyond any sense perception. They constitute what is famously described as Karmas and no body can escape their impact here or hereinafter. That is the cosmic law and that is also science. A person may die a physical death, but his Karmas will not dissolve in thin air and will cause to give pain or pleasure, happiness and sorrow, wealth and penury at the appropriate time.

There exists a symbiotic relationship between life-Karmas-death-rebirth. A person's karmas will decide the kind of life he will lead in this birth or the next. In fact, they also have a bearing upon the changes in the form of the living organism all of us are subjected to, in our birth-death cycle. This fact may have been borrowed from the scriptural knowledge, but that does not diminish its value or significance one bit. There is knowledge beyond the senses, and if our past experience and inferential knowledge does not contradict it, it is deemed to be a proof.

In many ways, ignorance of this fact or non-belief in the cycle of constant and an unending chain of birth and death, create favourable conditions for the preservation of the universe in the present form. The cosmic energy that keeps the entire universe intact and cohesively bound operates on the principles of duality. There is no neutrality in any of the phenomena that take place in the universe. The principles of duality also govern the phenomenon and indeed, the principle of relativity. No body in the modern context is unfamiliar with the relative nature of all events that affect the mankind in a holistic sense. Also, it is not a surprise that the theory of relativity, in its climatic manifestation found its expression in cosmic energy. Albert Einstein's famous formula $E=mc^2$,which is about mass, energy and speed, finally led to the production of atom bomb whose destructive effect was witnessed by the world during the Second World War. This was also the basis of another weapon of massive and bigger destructive potential, the nuclear bomb that shifted from the concept of fission to fusion. The fusion, two opposites coalescing into each other, can generate power of unlimited potential and perhaps assume the shape of cosmic energy.

The same energy, if harnessed properly and used in a constructive manner can improve the lives of millions of people on this planet. This cosmic energy, operating at different levels and places is responsible for maintaining this universe in the shape that we find it in, as also for generating the wherewithal for the survival of all living organism.

The power of fusion is demonstrated by a celestial event as well. The phenomenon of shakti entering into Shiva creates the power that he wields, when the universe is ready for dissolution and is on the throes of destruction. Shiva without Shakti is a mere Shava, a dead body, but his tandav nritya is a manifestation of that energy which is produced by the phenomenon of fusion.

Interestingly, the same phenomenon forms an integral part of the Vedanta philosophy. Advaitvad, the corner stone of this philosophy means non-duality and represents the fusion of the opposites and the inevitable presence of the fountainhead of this cosmic energy in the form of what we commonly call God. In other words, wherever the two opposing forces meet and completely fuse into each other, rendering their independent identity irrelevant, we will discover God. He therefore, represents the ultimate power, like the one generated by nuclear fusion. The power of God or the Supreme energy is pure and is indeed, responsible for keeping this universe in the state that we find it now or, shall, millions of year later. That is the *Samatava bhav*, unchangeable, unaffected and unruffled. It is beyond any attributes and has no properties of its own.

The Bhagwad Gita in Chapter 2, Shloka 38 says the following:

Sukh Dukhe Same Kritva
Labha Labho Jaya Jayo
Tato Yudhaya Yujyasva
Naivam Papam Vapsyasi

"Treat happiness and sorrow, profit and loss, victory and defeat on the same footing. Fight the battle of your life and you will commit no sin".

Indeed, that will also prepare a person to attain union with the Supreme force.

There lies a difference in the material and the cosmic or shall we say the spiritual world. The fusion of matter and anti-matter will generate enormous energy which if not harnessed properly can lead to the destruction of the world. The same energy in the hands and control of the Supreme force that is known to us as God operates this universe with clockwork precision and provides benevolent sustenance.

Krishna reiterates this *Samatva Bhav* in Chapter 2, Shloka 48 as follows:

Yogasth Kuru Karmani
Sangam Tyaktva Dhananjya
Sidhyasidhyo Samo Bhutva
Samatvam Yog Uchayate

"One, who remains detached maintaining perfect equanimity in success or failure, is a Yogi and said to be situate in Samatva Bhav".

One of the important messages of the Gita relates to maintenance of perfect equipoise in the face of adversity and happiness. Ordinary humans get greatly excited and often go overboard when they get what they had aspired for, especially in the material sphere. When some adverse situation hits them, they drown themselves in the cauldron of inconsolable misery. The dual nature of this universe will ensure that happiness and misery will keep visiting every resident of this world at different intervals. At no point in time, same situation will persist for a long while and both situations will take their turns in affecting people and the universe. Phenomena of life and death, is also an offshoot of this syndrome. It is therefore necessary to deromanticize death, regard it as any other event that must necessarily take place in the life of all and shed any fears of its arrival.

Every one has to die a physical death one day, is a thought that must remain with all of us, without giving it an undue importance. This world comprises largely good people who wish to lead a happy and a comfortable life without trespassing on others' life. If everybody is allowed adequate freedom to pursue the course of life they have chosen for themselves, the world would carry on without any major upheavals. Relative peace and calm would prevail and every one would continue to co-exist with their fellow beings, in an environment marked with joy and camaraderie. But in reality, the actual picture is starkly different, primarily on account of our uncontrolled desires that are based more on greed than our legitimate needs.

One of the ancient scriptures of Indian thought, Yajurveda has spelt out some thoughts on this subject in Ishavasyopanishad as follows:

> *Ohm Ishavasyamidam Sarvam*
> *Yatkinch Jagatyam Jagat*
> *Ten Tyakten Bhunjitha*
> *Ma Gridh Kasya Swidhanam*
>
> *"The entire universe is marked with the presence of the Supreme force called Ish and belongs only to Him. Take only that which is given by Him according to your needs. Do not lust on others' share and be content with whatever is given".*

Contrary to this profound advice that is meant to create peace and tranquility all around, some of us allow our greed to prevail upon our normal nature and we deliberately start encroaching upon the share that is meant for others. This initiates an avoidable bedlam, leading to a vicious circle where each one is trying to take away what belongs to others. Our material aspirations, unfortunately cloud our vision and we join an unending race of appropriating the world for ourselves as if there is no tomorrow. Suddenly, death strikes and all our material possessions earned by dubious means are left behind. This results in a kind of double jeopardy. We earn bad name for our misdeeds and are also rendered incapable of making use of our ill-gotten wealth.

Death snatches away everything that belongs to us, including that which has been earned by illegitimate means and levels up everything. Death repudiates all claims to the material possessions for ever.

Some of us sometime are able to hide our ill-gotten wealth from one of the most dreaded entity on earth, the tax man. Try as hard as you may, you will not succeed in doing it from death.

Lack of awareness about death, and a false sense of immortality that some of us are afflicted with creates another set of undesirable people. They possess an evil disposition and are a cause of immense misery to their fellow beings, while they are alive. They would inevitably cause some grief to those that are close to them, at the time of their death. They would also continue to cause problems, long after they are gone. The last bit happens on account of conflicting claims on the ill-gotten wealth that they had amassed during their lifetime. Such people are veritable pests of society. It is true that no one ever expects to die and no one ever anticipates it, least of all those who possess an evil streak. No one therefore consciously prepares for it, resulting in long drawn fights and squabbles on the legacy left by them.

Full knowledge and awareness of death is therefore absolutely essential. It is extremely important to prepare for it without waiting for it though. Nobody has been able to predict the exact time of one's death. It comes unannounced and generally when one least expects it. Prudence and love for your own people, demands that you adequately prepare yourself for it and do not become a cause of avoidable rift long after you are gone.

Chapter 8

Death and Cosmic Energy

"We are the product of this vast cosmos and dissolve into it."

In any part of the world, whenever we wish to thank God for His mercy, we raise our hands and look up. Interestingly, we see nothing but the vast emptiness completely enveloping us all around. We see the sky that exists only notionally. At night we see the stars and moon millions of miles away. Somewhere up there, we are also looking for the most elusive entity known as God. No body till date in the recorded history has seen Him yet and not likely to, in the near or distant future. Man has landed on moon and apparently, he has also not given evidence of any sightings of anything that looks like God. Further up, from Mars or Jupiter where man may land in future, chances of sighting that entity seem utterly doubtful. Landing at Sun, an utterly impossible occurrence which could have facilitated His 'Darshan' appears entirely impossible phenomenon.

For millions of years, this practice of looking skywards has been going on and will perhaps continue in the same form and in the same statuesque style. Why does a man pretend to look at apparent nothingness? Where is his scientific rational mind that allows him to perform an act that is as futile as it is ludicrous?

Krishna makes a very interesting observation that might provide some lead to this behaviour. In Chapter 9, Shloka 6 he says the following:

Yathakash Sthito Nityam
Vayu Sarvatrago Mahan
Tatha Sarvani Bhutani
Matsthani Iti Updharya

"Entire universe and humanity is installed in Me the same way, as the air that is present in, and situated all over the sky".

The vastness of this universe in size and potential, the celestial bodies, the brightness and energy of the Sun not only overawes us immeasurably it also shows us our rightful place, literally and metaphorically. We are, and feel like a speck, a tiny dot and an infinitesimal fraction of all natural creations. This cosmos is absolutely beyond any sense perception and the power and fury of natural events is completely incomprehensible to human intellect and unmanageable, notwithstanding spectacular technological prowess in the hands of mankind.

Man may have made impressive strides in the field of science and technology. He may have also succeeded in taming several minor forces and indeed, transformed them to serve his own needs. But he is still a small speck in front of the boundless power of numerous cosmic phenomena and cosmic energy which when unleashed, has the potential to destroy half of mankind, if not more.

Somewhere deep within, we all know it and are fully aware of it. Some of us may not openly acknowledge it though. That is why whenever, something of an incomprehensible magnitude occurs or we experience a sense of awe, we raise our hands instinctively seeking His benediction and protection. Also, when we achieve something spectacular, we look up to thank Him for His grace. We are instinctively led to believe that God is somewhere up in heaven, a beautiful colony many miles above the fictional sky. This is despite the fact that both sky and heaven exist only in our consciousness and do not exist in reality. In fact, God, heaven and hell all exist right here on this earth, within and without.

The sum total of energy, kinetic and potential in the cosmic context is infinite and there is no scale yet invented by man that can measure it. All of us are an integral part of it, and just by our existence in the universe and by our actions, we add to, or subtract from the total cosmic energy on a continuous basis. We create our own heavens and hells by our own karmas.

It would be interesting to define our existence in the language of this cosmic energy, and that will help to create a clear perspective of our position vis-à-vis the universe. It will also to an extent, solve the mystery attendant upon our frequent births and deaths in the world. This world comprises matter that is seen by us in three different forms, solid, liquid and gas. There is also a fourth state known as ether that is accepted in the metaphysical space but physicists of the world are wary of it, because of lack of concrete visual evidence that can be tested in the laboratory. Although the scientists of yore did accept its presence, the modern rationalists are little skeptical about its presence in the universe. Be that as it may, each particle of matter contains energy, either in kinetic or in the potential form. A simple distinction can be drawn from a piece of wood which, if thrown by an external force will exhibit kinetic energy. The same piece of wood, if lying undisturbed will have potential energy hidden inside in the form of fire. This piece of wood, if ignited will generate energy but till such time it happens its energy will only remain potential. A broad distinction is in the static and the dynamic nature of the matter.

All bodies in the universe, whether in the living form or inanimate form including the celestial ones are composed of matter. Break them into tiny pieces and they will all have molecules, atoms, electrons, protons and a nuclear body around which they revolve. They all possess energy of one kind or another. These atoms and molecules in a combination of their own ilk or of another kind, keep on breaking and coalescing continuously at a breakneck speed and produce resultant energy. In this process they are also responsible for creating several objects, some of which create a visual impact. Frequencies at which they evolve are of varying degrees and therefore, they also create objects that are not visible to the naked human eyes, which are conditioned to see objects only in a specific frequency range.

Formation and creation of all living organism, bears a close resemblance to the process and phenomenon described above that also governs the creation and destruction of all other objects including the celestial ones. Human beings comprise what is commonly known as "Panchbhoot". They are born and created by a combination of five elements, and on their death dissolve into these five elements to be created again. All that is required to construct him is sourced from here and on demolition it goes into the debris from where, by a complex procedure of reengineering, it is retrieved again for a new shape and a body. This is how the universe goes on and indeed, has been going on for aeons. It will go on like this for ever and ever. The phenomenon of nemesis or the fable of Noah's ark falls completely in the realm of mythology, and it is patently unscientific to presume or believe that the end of the universe can ever occur. It is absolutely impossible.

"Panchbhoot" that were described above refer to five elements that are, earth, fire, water, air and ether. These are all natural elements that are available in an elementary form, and in abundance. The task of the Creator has thus been made easy, because of the ready availability of all the required raw materials and there is no restriction on its supply. He must have had some contingency plans for meeting large orders from countries like China and India and made his preparations accordingly. God, apart from several other attributes must also be credited with enormous anticipation and foresight.

All these elements in their primal state or in collaboration with one or more elements must also mean energy. The combination of five elements would evidently, mean much more energy than what an individual element will command. In other words, we are a bundle of energy grown out of five basic elements and indeed in real sense, it is this latent energy that makes us perform all our functions. Our relationship with nature and the external universe is also symmetrical and that facilitates an easy assimilation of all that is required to keep the fire of energy burning. Again, the five elements that make us up are exactly the same that are available in abundance outside of us. The air for breathing, earth for food supply, fire for cooking, water for cleansing and ether, that provide perfect coordination amongst all these needs and functions.

This situation must also lead to an inevitable conclusion that whatever is inside us is exactly the same that is outside of us, in terms of the nature and character. It will of course be foolhardy to hazard a guess about their quantum.

This reality was known to the seers of Vedanta philosophy who therefore coined the famous "Mahavakya", Aham Bramhasmi which translated literally means, I am the God. That is the true identity of all living beings. They are indeed the true manifestation of God and an integral part of cosmic energy which is another formless form in which He exists. In scientific parlance this would mean the following:

> *"All elements that are present in the universe are also present in our body in the same proportion as our body's proportion to the universe".*

This should really be axiomatic. It cannot be otherwise. Just as an obvious illustration, our body comprises two-thirds of water and rest is the body mass consisting of all known elements like, oxygen, hydrogen, carbon, potassium, sodium et al. Our planet has the same proportion of water and the rest is present in an elementary state.

Interestingly, the classic definition of Yoga is joining the two, and these two refer to the external and internal. Creating a state of perfect harmony and balance between the inside and outside of the body is what Yoga is all about. Whenever, there is disharmony or variation in the prescribed levels of water and other elements in the body, we feel physically unwell. We are aware of the effects caused by long periods of dehydration. We have heard of serious problems caused by sodium or potassium deficiencies. Or conversely, Yoga is an art by which we seek to keep these compositions at an optimum level. Our body and mind must remain completely in sync with the elements of external nature.

We must now look at some special properties of energy, and that will give us some insight into the phenomenon of birth and death. The two prominent properties of any form of energy are its indestructibility and its inter-convertibility in another form. It is common knowledge that energy exists in a variety of forms. We know of electrical, mechanical, sound, and nuclear and wind energy. Important point to note is that the energy is the same, but it manifests itself in different ways. It is essentially power that lights a lamp, helps us speak, makes us walk, flies an aircraft and moves a huge ship. From movement of a tiny particle to running a colossal vessel, it is the effect of that ubiquitous energy that pervades and controls all movements in this universe. One form of energy is constantly converting itself into another form. That is where the distinction between the potential and kinetic energy becomes relevant. All forms of potential energies ordinarily lie dormant, unless an external source of another form of energy is applied to it which changes its form into kinetic. All forms of kinetic energies are constantly changing and are subjected to the dynamics of inter-convertibility.

Another unique feature of energy is that it never dies and never disappears. In fact the first principle of physics relates to the concept of indestructibility of energy in its aggregate form. It may appear to dissipate marginally because of the intervention of other forces that are at work, like friction caused by air and earth, but its quantum in the universe remains unchanged forever. It may seem to vanish from here for a while, but would at the same time appear elsewhere in the same or another form, keeping its quantum intact.

Energy as an integral part of this cosmos inevitably, follows all the immutable principles of nature. One of them being the dual nature of all entities, energy also exists in a dual form to create an impact. It does not exist in a neutral form. It manifests itself as negative and positive, yin and yang, male and female. It assumes power only, when the two opposites join together to build up a system, by which we are able to make use of it in a variety of ways that we do.

Let us go back to our earlier assertion of the man being constructed out of Panchbhoot, five elements that exist in the universe with an abundant supply. All these five elements represent a form of energy. Bringing them together, and making of a human being through a complex procedure known only to nature or the Supreme energy, requires energy of some dimensions. The product of this exercise, which is the human being, is also a form of energy. Indeed a closer examination of this entity called human being will reveal that he seems to possess all kinds of energy, like sound, electrical, mechanical and wind.

A man in every sense of the term, in other words, is energy, a bundle of energy. The quantum of energy in two individuals will vary, but each one is composed of energy and is energy personified. Let us now apply to this entity, the unique properties of energy that we discussed above, and we will not find it difficult to understand the phenomenon of life and death. All energies in a human being keep interacting continuously at an alarming speed, causing wear and tear to the material that the body is composed of. The body must necessarily reach a stage where the containment of different forms of energies, in a shell that has been considerably weakened by several forces, becomes unsustainable and it seeks dissolution back into its source, the Panchbhoot. This is the stage when death occurs to the body.

Life and death therefore really means conversion of one form of energy into another and that must happen inevitably, because of the intrinsic characteristics of the primal energy of which the entire living organism is composed. The same analysis leads to another interesting and a known phenomenon, which is that none of the living organisms ever die a permanent death. It only temporarily changes and remains present in another form to be renewed again. Let us add to this incontrovertible scientific fact, a scriptural knowledge of the existence of soul and the picture about the entire cycle of birth and death, and other related phenomena becomes complete.

The cycle of life-death phenomenon therefore really involves the following:

1. Existence of energy in the universe.
2. Using this energy on joining the five elements present in the universe to create a human being, a bundle of energy.
3. Use of energy by human beings in a variety of ways to live his life.
4. Its gradual dissipation in the face of natural elements till its containment in one human body becomes unsustainable.
5. Its dissolution into the vast reservoir of energy and becoming an integral part of cosmic energy.
6. Rejuvenation of energy for creation of a new body out of the aggregate cosmic pool.

Life and death really signifies regeneration, dissipation and rejuvenation of energy, all phenomena being sourced from the matter available within the universe.

Chapter 9

Life-Death-Life, A Continuum

"A journey from the finite to infinite."

Our universe is a big huge ball of cosmic energy comprising celestial objects like the Sun, Moon, Jupiter and all other planets, some known and some unknown. It has millions of stars, some of them reputed to be even bigger than the biggest planet known to mankind. These are all scattered in different parts of the galaxy and chances of exploring all of them by the human race seems well-nigh improbable, if not impossible.

Then there are multiple material objects present in the universe and in possession of potential energy that have been in existence for millions of years. Some of them have perhaps, remained in the same state for several thousand years and many of them have undergone changes in size and location, by the application of massive force of energy. The reference is to mountains, rivers, glaciers and several human habitations that have, over a period of time undergone momentous changes.

Thousands of civilizations are known to have evolved, progressed and declined, and then completely disappeared from the face of earth. Similar changes must have taken place at other celestial locations in the universe, of which the mankind on earth is unaware. Archeologists of the world have very meticulously, mapped the history of many civilizations on the basis of ruins discovered by them from time to time.

On a similar strain, human beings have also evolved from their primal state, either as apes or humanoids and assumed the present shape. The work done by several anthropologists will bear testimony to these facts. It is certainly not the end of these phenomena, and no body can argue with absolute conviction and knowledge that more changes will not take place. In other words, the entire universe and its inhabitants, animate or inanimate will continue to grow and decline inexorably. There are good chances that the manner in which human beings die and are born again, in a stipulated time frame, other objects also experience a make-over, albeit within a longer time frame.

A simple observation will tell us that there are two very basic traits of Nature. One, that it is absolutely impartial to all its creations, and two, it subjects all the objects in its womb to a constant process of evolution and involution. This indeed is the inherent nature of the Nature. The longevity of each of its creations, of course varies. We may add one more phenomenon, typical of this universe that it operates completely on the basis of dynamic principles. To remain static is not part of its inherent nature.

Krishna had explained in great details, the entire cycle of births and deaths, of destruction and regeneration to Arjuna. The permanence of all living entities in different forms, down the ages is repeatedly emphasized by Him in the course of His discourses in the Gita. Convinced about the imperishability of his soul and his continued presence in this universe, Arjuna has certain doubts about several lives he must necessarily spend in this world before he is freed from this bondage and attains Moksha.

There is an interesting dialogue and an exchange of questions and answers in Chapter 6 of the Gita. These are contained in Shlokas 37 to 45 and are reproduced below:

Ayati Shradhya Upeta
Yogat Chalitmanasa
Aprapya Yogsansidhim Kamam
Gatim Krishna Gachati 37

Arjuna asks Krishna, "Tell me about the fate of a person who is a yogi but can not exercise control on his senses and towards the end of his life, strays from his path. What happens to him?"

Kaschit Na Ubhayvibrashat
Chhinabhram Iv Nashyati
Apratishto Mahabhao
Vimudho Bramana Pathi 38

Arjuna further asks, "Does that person pursuing a spiritual journey is torn asunder like a cloud because of a few misdemeanors on his part?"

Atat Me Sanshyam Krishna
Chhetum Aharsi Asheshta
Tvadnay Sanshasya Asaya
Chheta Na Hi Upapadyate 39

Arjuna pleads with Krishna and "implores him to clear his doubts about an issue that concerns every living being, He adds that there is no one more competent than Krishna who can throw light on this subject".

Clearing Arjuna's doubts about an issue that affects all imperfect beings, Krishna tells him the following:

Partha Naiveh Na Mutra
Vinasha Tasya Vidhyate
Na Hi Kalyankrit Kaschit
Durgatim Tat Gachhati 40

Krishna very reassuringly tells Arjuna that "Such yogi who is generally engaged in pursuing a spiritual path with devotion is never destroyed, neither in this life or hereinafter".

Prapya Punya Kritam Lokan
Ushitva Shashvati Sama
Shuchinam Shrimatam Gehe
Yogbhrasht Abhijayate 41

"A person momentarily misled from his mission avails himself of all the good deeds that he has performed and thereafter is born in the household of people with good conduct and pure heart".

Athva Yoginam Aiv
Kule Bhavati Dhimtam
Aitadwi Durlabtarm Loke
Janam Yat Idhrasham 42

"Or else such a person is born into the families of yogis and people with great wisdom. Such births in this world undoubtedly, are very rare".

Tatra Tam Budhisanyogam
Labhte Paurvdehikam
Yatate Cha Tato Bhuya
Sansidho Kurunandana 43

"In his new birth, he on his own acquires the Samskaras of his previous birth and under their combined influence, works much harder in pursuit of his spiritual mission".

Purvabhyasen Tenaiv
Hriyate Hi Avasha Api Sa
Jigyasu Api Yogasya
Shabd Braham Ativartate 44

"With the support of his past karmas, that misguided yogi without any doubt, transcends the bonds of bad karmas and resumes the path of liberation".

Pratyanat Yatman Tu
Yogi Sanshudhi Kilbhisha
Anekjanam Sansidh
Tato Yati Param Gatim 45

"Yogi who is constantly engaged in pursuing a path of absolute devotion, attains Moksha in this birth on the strength of the cumulative effect of his past karmas".

Bhagwad Gita, a repository of great knowledge and wisdom, reproduces the words of one of the most enlightened and revered personages in the history of Vedic thought. Krishna has no peers in the field of spiritual practices, management of one's life and indeed, is regarded as God incarnate. We are all constantly engaged in search of truth, and when that truth is available to us through the authority of that supreme energy that controls the entire universe, it is foolhardy to question its meaning and relevance.

In Chapter 4, Shloka 5, Krishna responding to the doubts of Arjuna about the cycle of life and death says:

Bahuni Me Vyatitani
Janmani Tav Charjuna
Tani Aham Ved Sarvani
Na Tvam Vetha Prantapa

> *"O Arjuna! I and you have lived several births. You do not know any of them but I know them all".*

All our scriptures and the spiritual thought have absolute convergence on the issue of continuous cycle of life and death and rebirth. No body really goes away from here. What actually perishes and becomes invisible is just a body, which any case is made out of what is available here and goes back to it, only to seek renewal. That renewal may happen in any one of the living forms that exist in the universe. This would depend upon what we have done, our karmas in the previous live or lives. This is where the significance of the Gita's message comes in. It time and again, emphasizes on real identity of all living beings, which does not consist of the physical body, which in all events is impermanent. Our real self is represented by our soul which is pure and eternal and really is integral part of the Supreme energy known to us as Parmatma. This soul in spiritual parlance is called Atma. Interestingly, even the western thought which does not believe in the incidence of life after death or in the cycle of death and birth, accepts the word soul as an essential part of English dictionary and indeed, uses it extensively in their routine conversation. While they recognize it as a myth, Indian and Eastern philosophy accepts it as a reality. The soul does not have a body, is subtle in nature and is a subject only of perception in the same way as is God. God does not have a body. In fact, Vedanta thought describes God as Nirguna Nirakar, an entity that does not have any shape or any characteristics. Atma, the soul that is an integral part of Parmatma, the God and like Him is also an entity of perception and does not have a body, like the whole of which it is just a part.

We are here in this universe for ever and this fact, indeed a truth must be accepted gracefully by all concerned. Without being judgmental about any other divergent thought, it must be stated that it is only a short term view of our existence that creates several incidents of blatant inequity and disharmony in the universe.

Having recognized our place in the universe, we now need to be clear about our objective. We could spell out many and each one may be relevant from the individual standpoint. For the lesser creation of this universe, the animal world, one clear objective would be survival and to meet that objective, killing others to survive is also acceptable. Nobody punishes a lion for killing a deer for his own survival. For human beings, clearly presumed to be the superior creation and enjoying the benefit of intellectual prowess far superior to animals, the objective must necessarily be something higher. Here also different perceptions will proclaim variable objectives, depending upon the priorities everyone sets for himself and the level of their spiritual thought. It may be difficult to seek convergence of thought on this issue, even amongst highly enlightened souls. Different philosophical and spiritual streams spell out different goals, and that perhaps is one reason why large chunk of humanity lives an ordinary existence and leaves without making any difference to the universe. They do not even discharge their normal debt to this universe, of having availed of several benefits that are conferred upon them free of cost.

Frequent arrival in, and departure from, this universe is somewhat like a tenant renting out space here from the master of the universe. He uses all the comforts of living from this universe and it stands to reason that he must pay it back in some form. How many of us do that and in what manner? How many of us even think about it as an obligation that must be discharged? There have to be certain acceptable ways by which we please the landlord of the universe, or at least satisfy Him for our redemption. Both these questions relating to the agreed objective, and the manner in which we must attain them and pay back our debt in the process, are interlinked and we must seek an answer to them. Wherever there is a large congregation of people, there would be several opinions and hence several objectives, a hierarchy of objectives. Let us list out some of the possible ones.

A large majority of humanity would opt for objectives that fall within the province of the material. Some would want wealth and fame, some would ask for power and glory and others would want a life of happiness and fulfillment. A few wise people would prefer to lead a life of contentment and peace. A small cross section of people would want to serve their fellow men and would be content with minimal personal needs. A handful of people would want to achieve something spectacular that may serve the mankind and would want to leave a name synonymous with success, and be remembered. There would also be some people who possess an evil streak and would only think of their own selfish needs, and would not hesitate in creating or causing trouble for others. This class of people, and majority would fall in this category, are clearly body-centric and are not able to see beyond this world and themselves.

A miniscule percentage of people would work tirelessly for the sake of work and would not bother about rewards of their work. They are true karamyogis. Some of these karamyogis would perform all their work in the service of humanity and offer everything to God, including surrendering themselves to His will. Such people are true men of God and do everything on His behalf, and for Him. Let us pause here for a while and ponder over the significance of their work and objective.

We have recognized and indeed, accepted each living being to be an integral part of that Supreme power called God, Parmatma. We are here in this universe and the world, because of Him, and as His representative. At some point of time we must go back to our source and merge our identity in Him. In reality, we have no other independent identity and are only His infinitesimal part. With this truth in our support, it should not be difficult to create a formulation for our objective, indeed for all living beings and the manner in which to achieve it.

> *The only objective of all living beings in this universe is to attain Him, and this must be done by performing all deeds in His service, for and, on His behalf. There is no other objective, indeed there cannot be, and no other way of getting there.*

This is exactly what Krishna is saying in the nine shlokas from Chapter 6 reproduced above. It is extremely important for all of us to understand our true identity, which does not fall within the domain of the physical. Whatever is physical, gross and visible is only transitory and is just a shell, an outer covering which must peal off in due course, or when it reaches its expiry date. Our true vocation is to verily attain Him and thus get out of this bondage of the cycle of life and death.

Krishna makes an unequivocal declaration of our objective and tells Arjuna to strive for attaining Him by selfless work, dedication, worship and ultimate surrender to Him and only Him. He tells Arjuna to pledge his body, mind and intellect to Him and he will undoubtedly reach Him. Death or the fear of death ceases to have any meaning in that situation. Arjuna expresses certain doubts about his own capacity to constantly remain engaged in good karmas. Realizing the weak nature of us mortals, who despite performing good karmas, are vulnerable to scores of temptations present in this world full of Maya. Even the highly enlightened ones are prone to fall from their avowed path sometime.

There is a famous anecdote, oft-repeated in social circles pertaining to a sage Vishwamitra who was an enlightened personality and happened to be Guru of Rama, another highly revered figure in Hindu mythology. Vishwamitra, on the strength of his yogic powers and dedicated worship to the lord, gained enormous aura and the kingdom of gods presided over by Indra felt threatened. Somebody whispered to him about Vishwamitra's intentions of dislodging him from his position as the king of gods and goddesses. Indra, evidently fearing the loss of his eminent position as the head of his kingdom, hit upon a plan to extenuate the impact of Vishwamitra's powers acquired through dedication and worship of the lord. He chose the most beautiful woman in his kingdom by the name of Menaka and asked her to go down where Vishwamitra was performing his worship. The objective was to lure him from his chosen path of worship that could confer upon him unlimited powers including, the power to dislodge Indra. Menaka, following the orders of her master went where Vishwamitra was sitting and did all that was required to seduce him. Vishwamitra fell to the charms of that seductress and perhaps committed a few indiscretions. This had the effect of his power being considerably diluted resulting in Indra's throne remaining unchallenged.

Vishwamitra may not have succeeded in occupying the throne that had been the exclusive preserve of Indra, but his name and reputation in spiritual space remains absolutely intact. He was quick to realize that his conduct was certainly not consistent with the spiritual journey that he was traversing and had to make amends for it. He went back a few steps and lost out on the precious time, but worked much harder on the strength of his past karmas to seek realization.

Echoing similar views, Krishna is quick to dispel Arjuna's doubts and tells him that none of his good karmas are washed away by one or two acts of indiscretions. Nothing is wasted in the spiritual world and on the contrary, on the strength of his good karmas, he is born into the families of yogis and spiritually inclined people and is further inspired to carry on his efforts with renewed vigour.

In fact, this episode also brings out another feature that describes the contrary situations that exist between the spiritual and the material space. In the material world, for instance, you may perform several good deeds, but one small indiscretion that goes against the established norms of the society, is enough to bring down your reputation for ever. In that respect, spiritual world is more just and reasonable and it recognizes the fact that no human being is absolutely perfect and due allowance is granted to his imperfections. One can literally rise from the ashes if one has the will to purge oneself. This is somewhat like the concept of purgatory that some sects in the Christian faith subscribe to. Do not condemn a person for one or two mistakes and give him an opportunity to reform himself by committing penance and resuming the virtues of life.

We can draw a perfect analogy from the way educational system is structured in our world. You make an entry into the lowest of classes when you start your education. You do not gain admission in class tenth straightaway. You have to work for it and slowly year after year, you get promoted to the next level. From school, you move into a college, then to a university and gradually you graduate and reach the highest level of an independent research. You are then considered competent to charter your own path and are expected to contribute something original to your area of specialization. All this takes time, hard work and patience. There are of course, some exceptions where a precocious child manages to jump a few classes and reach the highest level faster than others. There are, in the same breath, some who either because of negligence or lack of adequate application fail in their class and take much longer to reach the highest level. There are some who never reach there and abandon their studies midway. Notwithstanding all this, nobody is able to take away the benefit of the class that has already been cleared. You therefore, start building up anew from the level that you have already reached, and despite the setback of your failure, work harder this time around to move on to the next level.

Interestingly, in the material sphere it is only the gross part of your existence and possession that either dies or is taken away, and not the subtle possessions like your good name, education, knowledge and wisdom. Your wealth and property, for which you may have squandered enormous time and energy, can be snatched away in few moments. Gross can not be reclaimed in your new birth, but a serious inquiry needs to be made into the fact whether the subtle acquisitions of a person in his previous births remain with him in some way. The Gita seems to suggest that we do and the expression used is "by Budhisanyoga" in Shloka 43 of Chapter 6. This really means that all our subtle acquisitions of past births, housed in our intellect and sub-conscious get carried over to our next birth. Judged from the standpoint of cosmic energy, this must happen for two reasons. Firstly, the total energy in the system remains the same always, and secondly, nothing in this universe is ever wasted. This phenomenon in the western thought is described as genes, while the oriental philosophy calls it Samskaras.

In the spiritual world as well, we take a few steps forward, as all of us must do and gradually move up the ladder towards our ultimate goal of going back to our source. In fact, that is how the entire universe and the living beings must operate. We all must go back to our source and that is where our redemption lies. Some of us will reach there faster than others, depending upon our karmas. Others, much like those who fail in their education space, must inevitably take longer. But everyone would reach there one day and till such time that happens, we will remain subjected to the repeated cycle of births and deaths.

All of us therefore, must listen to the voice of prudence and having set our eventual goal, work for reaching there as fast as possible. Our inbuilt imperfections and the web cast by Maya however, makes that much more difficult and delays the inevitable. The Gita gives the following counsel in Chapter 6, Shloka 5:

> *Udhret Atmana Atmanam*
> *Na Atmanam Avsadyet*
> *Atma Aiv Atmana Bandhu*
> *Atma Aiv Ripu Atmana*

> *"You must constantly strive to raise yourself and never let yourself be regressed. Man is his own best friend and his own worst enemy".*

These are indeed very profound words. You make your own destiny and you make it by making conscious choices. Nothing happens to anybody by chance, as that is neither spiritually nor scientifically sustainable. Whenever we come across any situation in life, we have several options (in fact, in reality there are only two). Our first reaction to all situations is generally based on truth and wisdom and that really is the voice of our soul, our consciousness which is pure and tenders the correct advice. It gives an advice that is in our interest and generates positive energy. We however, under the influence of our material desires and selfish interests, ignore it and follow the path that is both retrograde and against social norms. In time, that proves to be against our own interests as well. In that eventuality, we are quick to put the blame for our predicament on others, much of which is apportioned to God.

All of us face several challenges in our life and we react to them often, without much application or planning. Even in a normal situation, we are required to act to perform our duties.

There exists a constant conflict between our mind and intellect, one of which is based on emotions and desires, and the other that is founded on the strength of positive reasoning. It is usually the mind that wins and we get carried away and commit certain actions that are patently against our own and others' interests. All these factors therefore, ensure that we do not succeed in our mission in one life. We need many such lives and if we keep taking one step forward at a time, after discounting our imperfections, we will reach there. But for that to happen even after several lives, we shall have to lead a balanced existence all throughout. The pursuit of our material desires shall have to be properly tempered with, and not exhibit any extravagant behaviour at the expense of others.

Death is also described as an opportunity by the Gita to attain Him in this birth alone. It is interesting to reproduce following three Shlokas from Chapter 8:

Antkale Cha Mamev
Smaranmuktva Klevaram
Ya Pryati Sa Madbhavam
Nasti Atra Sanshaya 5

"There is no doubt that a person who has My name on his lips while breathing his last, attains Me".

Yamyam Vapi Smranbhavam
Tyajante Kalevaram
Tamtam Veti Kaunteya
Sada Tad Bhav Bhavita 6

"After death, a person attains the same state that he was in, at the time of release of his body because that was the state he had always remained during his life".

Tasmat Sarveshu Kaleshu
Mam Anusmar Yudhya Cha
Mayi Arpit Mano Budhi
Mam Aiv Aishyasi Asanshyam 8

Krishna advises Arjuna that "You should therefore constantly think of Me, worship Me and fight the battles of your life. Surrender your mind and intellect to Me and you shall doubtlessly attain Me".

Many great souls have known to have breathed their last with the name of God on their lips, and it is also a common belief that such people meet their creator very soon. Krishna confirms this belief in the shloka reproduced above. It is also important to understand that worshiping God is not a part time activity, something that is optional, to be engaged in at leisure or in the absence of any other occupation. It has to be an integral part of one's life. Only then will, one be able to remember His name at the last moment. That is why, in the 8th Shloka, Krishna tells Arjuna that he must think of Him always, "Sarveshu Kaleshu" and not only when it suits him.

No body could have expressed it better, and in simpler terms than Swami Ramakrishna Paramhansa. He once said that God has given us two hands. Keep doing your work with one and remember Him with the other. When you have finished your work, bring in the other and join both hands in His worship.

We are finite beings, but possess the power and potential to be, and meet the infinite. That really is our ultimate goal and each of our karmas must be designed to take us closer to that goalpost.

CHAPTER 10

Death in a Voluntary Mode

"Live your life for others and you shall die on your own terms."

We usually associate the event of death by intervention of external force and rightly so, because ordinarily no one wants to die and would hate to do anything foolish that may lead to a situation resulting in his death. On the contrary, our survival instinct is so highly developed that we shall consciously resist or avoid doing anything that is even remotely connected with the possibility of death. Our sixth sense, otherwise lying dormant suddenly comes to the fore as soon as, there is even the slightest hint of an impending danger or threat to our life.

This is the situation with majority of people and is an integral part of the evolutionary process. Normally people do not wish to die and would not voluntarily head towards it, or do anything that may lead to death. That is the rule. Like in all situations, there are exceptions to the rule and subject of death is no exception. There are following three/four situations where one knowingly becomes responsible for one's own death, in physical or in a metaphysical way.

1. All cases of suicide.
2. Committing a grave act of moral turpitude and getting exposed.

3. Indulging in an act or adventure, which is potentially very risky.
4. Protecting the integrity of one's motherland, of another individual and risking one's own life to save another.

Each of these four acts of voluntary nature has a different genesis and death resulting from each act, generates different kind of emotional reaction. The first two are steeped in crass negative behaviour and these deaths create an equally negative reaction. The third one can have mixed reaction from those affected by it or on hearing of it. The last one generates unqualified positive comments from the society and is unquestionably termed as death and sacrifice of the highest order.

We will begin with the last one. It is purely a voluntary act motivated by a strong commitment to certain basic values of human goodness, true understanding of one's Dharma, duty and responsibility as an enlightened citizen of this universe. Generally speaking, most of us lead our life on a very selfish plane, caring for our physical needs and leave this world without making a difference. If we have a family to support, we care for them and do whatever is possible to cater to their physical needs. The least ambitious amongst us have no other agenda in life. Those nursing an ambition for self-aggrandizement would work that much harder, but focus is entirely on the self. For such people, others do not exist and if anybody seeks their help, they would not stick their neck out, or go out of their way to extend a helping hand.

Then there are those who are fired with an ambition to serve the society, but they will condescend to do that only by keeping their personal interest above everything else. If by some effort, some public service gets delivered, they will happily go along. Politicians of the day would perhaps generally fall in this category. This is not to undermine the contribution of some politicians who have the interest of public at large, close to their heart and they work tirelessly towards that goal. But they also manage to appropriate power and several advantages to themselves at the cost of the nation. Politicians cannot normally, claim to perform absolutely selfless service. There are however, some with a vision and desire to lead the nation on the path of growth and development, but very few of them have known to have laid their life for any worthwhile cause. There of course, would be a few exceptions.

Every nation maintains a huge Army, Air and Naval force to guard against any violation of its territory. This is done in pursuance of its sovereign power and is recognized by every other civilized Nation. In a highly competitive world with several Nations nursing expansionist ambition, or because of historical reasons, frequent incursions sometime escalating to fierce battles or full-fledged war take place. Each Nation seeks to guard its territory with all the might at its command and this often results in casualties to its armed personnel. Men at the forefront expose themselves to the highest possible risk to their life and they do this voluntarily.

We have a growing army of cynics who would term these deaths as part of the duty and occupational hazard in which dead soldiers have no choice, but that is taking a very convoluted view of straightforward choice exercised by the soldier, knowing fully well that he may be called upon to lay down his life for the security of his country. Death of any armed personnel, in performance of his duties is the highest form of sacrifice and we cannot, and indeed should not allow anyone to belittle its importance. It is a kind of an offering of one's life in service of the nation. We need to salute these brave hearts.

Even during peacetime operations, many of our uniformed soldiers lay down their life so that rest of us live in peace. In modern societies, there are several groups of misguided people who consider violent means as the only solution to the disputes that are largely created on account of human avarice and lust for power. They have to be stopped in their tracks by use of force that can result in the death of soldiers with the state's authority. These deaths are also for a cause, and the martyrs are fondly remembered for their sacrifice.

We also come across many other instances, where a person not officially assigned the task of protecting ordinary citizens or public property, comes forward voluntarily and risk his life for a cause. Saving a drowning man or a child, or protecting the modesty of a woman in which there is a danger to one's own life, are examples of bravery rarely seen in the modern context where every body remains highly self-centered. Performance of such acts of bravery, not only calls for great self-belief, but also profound faith and concern for our fellow beings. Many people are known to have died in an attempt to save the life of people in distress. They have an option not to risk their life and be a by-stander like many others, but choose to do so, on the strength of their concern and values they cherish. They do that without expectation of any personal gain, and society must recognize their sacrifice and indeed honour them in their death. Incidents of this nature, serve to demonstrate to others, the goodness and courage of a few people and set an example for others to follow.

Death must come to all, sooner or later and if it comes for a cause, in which a person dies so that others can live on peacefully, it must be termed as the highest form of sacrifice. Unlike several deaths, these are not wasted.

Interestingly, we live in an exciting period of time, and with people of diverse cultures, values and ambitions. A large majority of people is busy chasing the necessities of life and living life in a state of peace and comfort. They live an ordinary life and die an equally ordinary death. There however, are a few who prefer to live life in a fast track and nurse ambitions of literally conquering the universe or at least making an attempt at that. They like to flirt with dangers and try doing things that would test the stamina and spirit of the most intrepid amongst us.

Ever since the creation of the universe, human beings have sought to overcome obstacles, taken up challenges and in a way tried to tame the natural forces and conquer the most difficult and treacherous of nature's creations. Technological advances made during the last two centuries, have only made him bolder and encouraged him to try the impossible. Reference is to those fired with the spirit of adventure, attempting to scale the highest peak or diving into the deepest point of earth, with an inherent risk to their life. We have examples of men and women traveling to the farthest point in the universe that technology can facilitate, and losing their life in an attempt to re-enter the earth's gravitational space. An Indian astronaut Ms. Kalpana Chawla is one such woman of grit and determination who lost her life doing exactly that. History of adventure sport is replete with numerous examples, where many people have lost their lives chasing a dream that many ordinary people would not even dare to dream. They may not lose their life in an attempt to save another life, but they do charter a course of journey others nursing a similar dream can learn from, and in that sense set an example.

Human beings have an inbuilt desire to set benchmarks of performance in the respective field of their endeavour and there are many others who seek to excel and raise the bar. Those who lose their life in pursuit of excellence pave a path for others to follow, and in that respect their sacrifice becomes part of history.

Deaths that take place in chasing an adventure are purely voluntary in nature and beckon the strong and intrepid ones, leave a legacy that others can learn from in similar pursuits and indeed, become exemplary. Mankind rightly registers them in the list of brave people.

Cosmic energy in this universe operates on the basis of duality and indeed every phenomenon takes place in a relative mode with equal positive and negative fall-out. In other words, while there are people who lay down their life performing good deeds for the benefit of others, there are some who either take others' life so that they can live or cause immense misery and hurt to others for their own pleasure. They commit heinous crimes, kill others, violate them and arrogate to themselves ugly power to satisfy their ego. By committing these acts, they are inexorably heading towards absolute infamy which for an ordinary respectable person means death. In fact, the rest of the society would wish them to die so that others can live in peace.

Every man's true nature is pure and is actually represented by his soul which is an integral part of the Supreme energy or God. No body envisions God as ugly or a criminal, indeed He is the most benevolent of us all. Those deviating from this path of virtuosity are treated as the wretches of society and their death is eagerly awaited, if not enforced by others. Those committing serious crimes or acts of grave moral turpitude are quietly condemned to death, even before the law of the land comes into operation.

Bad name and a spot on one's character, literally amounts to death. In fact, Krishna goes a step further and declares that anybody who tolerates injustice and refrains from performing his duty, his Dharma, is a coward and does not deserve to live. He delivers this statement while reminding Arjuna of his duty and tells him that if Arjuna does not rise and fight, the coming generations will call him a coward and for a respectable person that amounts to death. It would be worthwhile to reproduce here Shlokas 33 to 37 from Chapter 2, as follows:

Ath Chetvam Imam Dharmyam
Sangramam Na Karishyasi
Tata Swadharmam Kirtim Cha
Hitva Papam Avapsayasi 33

"If you do not fight this war being fought on certain principles, you will lose your reputation and good name and shall be termed a sinner".

Akirti Chapi Bhutani
Kathyishanti Te Avyayam
Sambhavitasya Cha Akirti
Marnat Atirichiyate 34

"Many people will talk about your disgraceful conduct for a long time and for a respectable person, bad name is worse than death".

Bhayat Ranat Upartam
Mansyante Tvam Maharatha
Yesham Cha Tvam Bahumata
Bhutva Yasyasi Laghvam 35

"Those who looked upon you with respect earlier would look at you with contempt, because they will presume that you ran away on account of fear".

Avachyavadan Cha Bahun
Vadishyanti Tav Ahita
Nindanta Tav Samarthyam
Tato Dukhtaram Nu Kim 36

"Your enemies will decry your valour and say many unmentionable things about you. There cannot be a greater sorrow than that".

Hato Va Prapsyasi Swargam
Jitwa Va Bhokshayse Mahim
Tasmat Utisht Kaunteya
Yudhyaye Krit Nishchaye 37

Krishna finally tells Arjuna, "If you are killed in this Dharamyudh, you shall reach heaven. If you win the war you shall rule the world. Therefore, O Arjuna! Stand up and prepare for a fight".

Performance of evil deeds or deliberate dereliction *of assigned duty leads to bad name, and that is death for any man who commands respect in society.*

These are incidents where the cause of death gets linked to person's own action committed overtly or covertly and is provoked strictly by voluntary actions and not thrust upon him by any external force. He may choose not to commit these acts, or in a parallel scenario, not shirk from his responsibilities. In that situation he need not anticipate death, well before his physical death. What is however, extremely important is to have a correct appreciation of one's duty created by the standard norms of society or linked with the vocation one has chosen for oneself. In the modern context when the lines amongst various classes of people are getting blurred, it is easy to decide on one's profession or calling in life. Having chosen it consciously, one should quickly understand the duties and responsibilities attached with it. Those duties inevitably, assume the status of one's Dharma and not performing them to the best of one's ability must invite condemnation. Unfortunately, some of us do not truly understand the range of our duties, leave alone performing them properly.

Interestingly, a closer study and examination of events that took place in an epic called Mahabharata, which occasioned the gospel of Gita reveals this truth. Krishna, standing in the middle of a cataclysmic war that was to change the course of Bharata's history, had his task cut out. Arjuna had laid down his arms under the influence of absolute depression and refused to fight his own kith and kin. Krishna realized that if Arjuna did not pick up arms and decided not to fight, Pandavs along with their entire army will be completely decimated and that would mean victory of evil over good. Kauravs's army was not an army of ordinary warriors. He could not be a silent spectator to that mayhem and injustice. Arjuna was equally convinced about his stance at not becoming the cause of death of his own close relations, Gurus, grandfather and host of friends with whom he had bonded all his life.

It took Krishna three hundred thousand spoken words, seven hundred shlokas and 18 chapters to explain to Arjuna his Dharma. He also had to tell, in unequivocal terms the consequences of Arjuna not performing his Dharma as a warrior. Abdication of one's Dharma, one's duties and responsibilities would bring in immense disgrace which signifies death for a person with honour. Doubts lingering in the mind of Arjuna were banished only after Krishna exhibited His own 'Viratswaroop' of an entity that was not of an ordinary mortal, but of God incarnate.

In other words, appreciation of one's Dharma and its performance to the best of one's ability alone means living one's life in a worthwhile manner. Conversely, those who do not, have never existed or lead a life no better that that of an animal.

Some actions that are strictly voluntary in nature, lead to a situation where the doer realizes his mistake and becomes extremely remorseful. He goes into depression, becomes elusive and in some extreme cases, decides to take his own life. This too is a death caused, purely by voluntary actions.

Oxford dictionary defines suicide as "the action of killing oneself deliberately". One comment that can be safely made about the incident of suicide, without any fear of contradiction is that no body can ever fully understand or know the real reason behind it. The person, who has committed suicide and achieved his objective of killing himself, is gone and every other testimony is only a secondary piece of evidence. This can, at best tell us only half the story. In fact, it might be difficult even for the person committing suicide to actually depose on the real reason for his deliberate act, because of a simple reason that while committing the act leading to his death, his cognitive and rational faculties are at the lowest ebb. There may be several reasons forcing him to take recourse to an extreme step which is entirely against his own nature, as also against the laws of nature.

One of the primary functions of nature relates to the process of evolution. Every body born in this world is expected to live his life fully, till age does him in. In order for him to do that successfully in absolutely hostile conditions, he has been equipped with strong survival instincts. It is this attribute that flies against any argument that suggests suicidal tendencies, as an offshoot of normal pressures of living. Survival instincts are so highly developed in all living beings that squeezing your own life, is both a physical and an intellectual improbability. During the course of living his own life, he is also expected to subscribe to the evolutionary requirements of nature and leave his seeds for germination. Contrary to this reality, some people openly defy nature and decide to take their own life. Just imagine if the first person born on this planet, had developed suicidal tendencies on the ground of utter loneliness or any other reason, we would not have seen the world in the form that we see it today.

Apart from the conflicts with the evolutionary theory, incidents of suicide cast a deep and dark shadow on the culture and the value systems of the society. Suicide does not remain an exclusive phenomenon limited only to the dead person, but reflects on the strength and character of the entire society. A society that creates human material of such propensities, followed by an unqualified condemnation of the resultant behaviour, would surely witness incidents of unnatural deaths on a large scale. Such societies are also conspicuously bereft of any organized counseling system, where people indulging in errant conduct can seek timely help and get over that impetuous rush of emotions leading to suicide.

There are some people who believe suicides to be simply psychopathological breakdown in the adaptive system. The depressed suicidal persons see themselve's as a burden to others, a blot on the society and are often made to think on those lines. That also to an extent explains, why suicides are concentrated heavily amongst the so called 'undesirables' in our society: the sick and infirm, the elderly, homosexuals and gender challenged, the financially bankrupt and those accused of moral turpitude.

People with strong suicidal tendencies may appear to be like any other normal human beings, but beneath the surface they are constantly fighting a losing battle with their self-esteem. One often comes across people with a high I.Q. succumbing to this unnatural way of terminating their life, for no obvious reason. One may go on endlessly trying to analyze the biology of suicides and its victims, but at the end of the day, each incident of this nature is unique to the person and has very specific reasons to it. This is one subject where any attempt at generalization would prove to be completely abortive. The only general statement that can be made about this phenomenon is that all suicides are unjustified, immoral and any society that directly or indirectly promotes it, or condones it is highly degenerate.

Most of us would be loath to allow the biology of suicide to work this way, and indeed, every humane person would do everything possible to prevent any one to resort to suicide as a means to seek redemption. Unfortunately however, we find that nature does not necessarily align itself fully with our own moral emotions.

On the spiritual yardstick as well, bringing an end to your own life by means other than those that are natural is absolutely unethical. We are all creations of nature and it is only that entity that has the right to terminate it, in the manner it deems fit. No human being can create another being (he can only reproduce it by a process designed by nature) and hence on the same analogy, no human being has the right to destroy it, including his own. Human beings are indeed the finest creation of nature, designed with a combination of most imaginative architectural engineering and a great aesthetic content. He has been given a pride of place amongst all living beings, and that has been done with a purpose. There are countless species of living beings and none can match the beauty, versatility and the power that a human being can wield. All living beings possess a body and means to look after it, with varying degree of efficiency. But each one has its own limitations circumscribed by the requirement of survival and just that. All other living beings have been performing these functions ever since they have existed and are not known to have done anything extraordinary. It is only man who is blessed with the body and a unique endowment called the intellect, which is capable of achieving the spectacular and an ability to constantly improve upon it. To waste it by a deliberate act is absolute insanity. Interestingly, suicide as a phenomenon takes place only in the human world. Animals or any other creation of nature is not known to indulge in this wanton act of self destruction.

Human beings possess an intellect that gives him the power of vision, imagination, will power, memory and the capacity to achieve the impossible. In spiritual parlance, while every living being is supposed to possess a soul, it is only man who is in a position to realize it and actualize it. In that respect he is not a mere body. He in fact, is a spiritual being, a store house of enormous power and potential that can bring him close to his creator and help him merge into Him. This is the ultimate goal of all living beings and the man is closest to Him. The core of Indian philosophical thought declares man as the rarest of rare amongst all living beings and announces that in that respect, he is the envy of gods and goddesses, who also have to be born as ordinary human beings to attain God. No body, least of all he himself has the right to cut short and destroy the opportunity of achieving the main purpose of his life.

Birth as a human being, according to the sages and the wise ones, comes only to those out of trillions of living beings, who have consistently performed good Karmas. It is an opportunity of a life time, nay an opportunity of several lives to pursue a path of goodness, service to others and take forward steps towards the ultimate goal. Every moment of our life has to be utilized with an eye on that objective and in doing everything that will take us closer to Him. No body should be wasting or destroying it either by negligence or by committing acts that are of evil nature, and hence retrograde. They will only take us many miles away from our creator, and to that extent make it difficult to attain Him.

Termination of one's own life with a deliberate act signifies cowardice, abdication of one's responsibilities and pushes an individual soul, miles backwards in the pursuit of his goal of merging with his creator. An act of suicide is no less a crime than that of a murder.

Chapter 11

Karmas—Life and Death

"We have control only on our Karmas and nothing else."

It is important to understand that all events pertaining to our life and death bear a direct relationship with the quality of our Karmas. Most of us ignore this fact at our own peril. While our Karmas have a strong and perhaps, the only determinant factor in facilitating the kind of species that we are born into, it also influences the factors like the family and parents that we are born to, and the place of our birth. It is also important to remember that nothing in this world ever happens by chance and our life and death are also determined by the choices we have made at different stages of our several lives that we live. These choices evidently translate into actions, speech and thoughts which really is the true definition of Karma. We would require some elaboration on this subject.

This world has trillions of living organism and at the current level, a few billions of human beings. This number keeps changing inter se, and my guess is that at any given point of time, the total number of aggregate living entities remains constant. It must be emphasized that this is purely a guess, and is based on one incontrovertible fact that the sum total of energy at a given point of time in the universe remains constant. All living beings, regardless of the species, are a veritable source of energy. Indeed, each one is a unit or units of energy and at an aggregate level, a part of the overall cosmic energy.

Both in the animal and human world, each individual are different from the other, even within their own specific group. We will however, confine our analysis on the human front. All human beings are physiologically identical or at least similar. Their body structure, external and internal organs are the same and perform same functions. In brief, all physical attributes just below the head level appear to be same and indeed, are same. There are different views about the shape and the content of brain, which according to researchers exhibits minor variations. But one can easily accept the argument that in physical structure and other physical endowments, nature has been absolutely impartial and has distributed its bounty evenly. It may have given certain special attributes to some people to weather extreme physical conditions, but that is a function more of the evolutionary expediency than an indication of initial intention at the time of distribution of assets to different living species.

Having stated this, it is also equally true, and can be stated without any fear of contradiction that no two persons are similar and indeed, each one is very different from the other in holistic sense. Two persons born to the same parents, receiving similar opportunities for growth and exposed to identical social milieu, exhibit vastly different reactions to similar situations and stimuli and possess different traits of character. One notices striking dissimilarities of temperament, behaviour and values, even amongst twins. How does one explain this divergence? This is one truism and we shall refer to it one more time later.

Let us look at another truth which perhaps is not so obvious, but a closer examination along with some keen observation will convince us of its validity.

In the life of every human being, there are only two things or events that are mandatory or inevitable and everything else that happens to him, or which is required to be done by him is either cosmetic or optional. These are:

1. Death.
2. Performance of Karma. Karmas will include thought, speech and action.

Inevitability and certainty of phenomenon called death, in the life of all does not require any enlightened discussion or convincing. Every one who is born must die to be renewed again, and this has been discussed in great detail in the preceding chapters.

The second and only other necessary and unavoidable phenomenon that must affect every human is Karma. No one can stay without Karma in this world, literally and metaphorically.

Krishna, in Chapter 3, Shloka 5 says the following:

> *Na Hi Kaschit Khshanmapi*
> *Jatu Tishtati Akarmkrit*
> *Karyate Hyvsha Karma*
> *Sarva Prakritijai Gunai*

> *"Undoubtedly, no body in this world, at any time can stay without work even for a moment. All human beings are compelled to perform Karmas by the influence of nature that has designed him such".*

Every living being is a bundle of energy and to sustain that energy that keeps him going, he constantly needs an extra bit. He must expend it and seek new quantum of energy. The only way he can acquire more energy, expend it and make a bid for fresh quantity, is to work. This he does by breathing, drinking and eating. In order for him to perform these functions of breathing etc. and live his life to the fullest he has to think, speak or act. In other words, in order to survive and live, he must perform karmas.

This is the inclusive part of the definition of karma. The exclusive component says that having been involved in Karmas as described above, a man need not do anything else. In other words, if he wishes to engage himself in any other pursuit, there is no restriction, but that other pursuit is completely optional and not essential for his survival. He has enough sustenance and the required quantum of energy from his Karmas and is quite comfortable without any additional intake.

Interestingly, our Karmas apart from providing complete sustenance to us also make us self-sufficient. Any other occupation is an add-on which is strictly optional. In fact, we are often misled when dealing with activities of optional nature and get into trouble. One can draw a simple comparison with our eating habits. A simple meal comprising barely sufficient nutrition is extremely healthy for us. Treat it as our Karma. We normally do not restrict ourselves to that and bring in lots of add-ons on our dinning table. This more often than not, gets us into trouble.

Another add-on that we bring in our life is to start worrying over the results of our Karmas. In fact, our preoccupation with the rewards of our karmas and efforts is so overpowering that our focus shifts completely from our karma to the reward, resulting in sub-optimal efforts and sub-optimal rewards. It cannot be otherwise. Receipt of less than expected reward, operates as strong disincentive to perform to the best of our ability. We either give up, or start resorting to karmas that are against our true nature, causing distortion in society and excess burden in our own life. For most of us, material wealth and prosperity becomes the sole aim for our existence and we tend to appropriate much more than we need and indeed, much more than we deserve. Our entire life revolves around our body and we do everything possible to make it comfortable, often at the expense of others. Our Karmas thus become the biggest casualty.

One must hasten to add that these statements are being made without being judgmental about the quality of karmas. Stating another truism, good karmas will give you good results and conversely, bad karmas will only create adverse effects. Any other situation is spiritually and scientifically, not tenable. Both kinds of karmas will generate corresponding kind of energy and at the appropriate time, you and you alone shall be the legitimate recipient of its impact.

Let us now create a mathematical model to establish the relationship between our Karmas and the life-death phenomenon. As stated earlier, every life has two variables that are of permanent nature, death and Karmas.

LIFE————KARMAS————DEATH

Death is common to all and therefore, can be deemed to be a neutral variable. That only leaves Karmas that must inevitably decide the course of our life. The quality of Karmas therefore, must decide the kind of life and indeed, the kind of death all of us get. Our choice is limited only to our Karmas and not to its result or consequences. Evidently you can choose only that which is in your hand and control. No body, however powerful in the history of the world has ever been able to completely achieve everything that he has set himself for, always. Many of course do so many times over, but to say that the results of their karmas are entirely in their control always, would be stretching the facts to an absurd level. Napoleon Bonaparte, famous French general, fought and won several battles. He was considered by many as almost unconquerable, till he met his waterloo at the appointed time.

If we jump from a ten-storey building, death would be painful and more or less certain, unless some miracle takes place. Jump from two storey building might just break a few bones. Result would be proportional to the quality of our Karmas.

Scriptural knowledge divides our Karmas in the following three categories:

1. Sanchit Karmas, karmas that we have performed overtime during the course of several births and are somewhat like a complete statement of the bank balance of Karmas, of each individual.
2. Prarabdh Karmas, that component of karmas that facilitate our birth in the human form and that which determines the quality of life we shall lead while we live.
3. Agami Karmas, karmas that we perform in this life and that which add on to the total balance of our Karmas in the sanchit category. These will influence the course of our future life.

The bank balance of karmas of an individual may be negative or positive, and that alone will determine his capacity to spend or live the life that he has created by his own karmas. The human form, the highest form in the echelons of the entire living organism would be available only to those that have a positive bank balance of karmas. If you take a large loan from the bank, or keep drawing heavily at regular intervals without ever paying back, your further capacity of drawls shall be frozen at some stage.

Additionally, you shall be required to pay a heavy penalty and an exhorbitant interest along with the amount that you have borrowed. Your living a life as human being becomes unsustainable, and you perhaps have to serve a sentence as some other inferior species out of several that are part of the living organism.

It must be clarified that there is no way that you can seek a temporary reprieve by borrowing from someone known to you and pay back part of your debt. Alternatively, if you were to steal to discharge your debts, you would only add further to your accumulated woes. Your karmas are strictly non-transferable and can not be traded with that of others. They are absolutely unique and specific to you and you alone shall have to be answerable for them. You can neither give nor take away any benefit accruing out of yours or others' karmas, at any time of your several long journeys in this universe. In the same logic, you cannot pass on the burden of your evil acts to others, nor will you take on others' burden.

Everyone's karmas are strictly non-tradable.

Interestingly, this fact was in a way responsible for Valmiki the famous dacoit who wrote Ramayana, the original epic narrating the story of Ram, undergoing complete transformation from a sinner to a saint. He was asked by the itinerant celestial bard known as Narad, whether his family members for whose upkeep and livelihood he has been killing people and earning money, are jointly responsible for his misdeeds. On receiving blatant refusal and a strong rebuff from his parents and other family members, Valmiki gave up his adventures and spent many years in the worship of the Supreme lord, acquired knowledge and wisdom only few could, and wrote an eternal epic Ramayana, one of the two most famous scriptures that several generations of Indians have cherished.

The essential components of Karmic thought, our own experience and observation of the experience that others go through, often raises certain legitimate doubts and questions about its validity. Why do good people not known to have performed evil deeds suffer? Why do rogues and scoundrels prosper and seemingly enjoy all the pleasures and comforts of this world and come to no harm? Why does a child of five years or less who has not had an opportunity to perform any karma, leave alone evil karmas, dies a painful death?

Let us attempt to analyze the situation in a holistic sense and seek answers to these apparent contradictions and mysteries of the universe where life, death and karmas are inextricably intertwined. Ordinarily, we are conditioned to seek a scientific proof of all events that take place in this universe, including those that fall within the province of strictly spiritual. We find hard to believe or accept anything that is not acknowledged by our senses or our intellect. But it is equally true that there is knowledge beyond the senses and anything that does not contradict reason and past experience, that knowledge is proof.

We will stick to our traditional approach of seeking scientific explanation to the queer phenomena, and apparently unanswerable questions listed above. We will then move into the spiritual space where we are armed only with the power of faith and where the evidentiary value of our thoughts is almost non-existent. This in many respects, shall be a unique way of seeking to reconcile two diametrically opposite areas of human concern. The precepts of science and spirituality, physics and metaphysics, material and celestial are completely opposite to one another. In seeking a convergence, we are trying to achieve the impossible, but the answers to the questions that we are looking for, are as difficult as they are necessary, for us to unravel the mysteries of the phenomena we are dealing with. Deal we must or else we shall all be following a blind alley of questions and answers without any enlightenment and without any need for improving our karmas for a meaningful existence.

We, in our endeavour are really trying to establish the validity of the Karmic principles. To begin with, we shall postulate the scientifically known or tested statements and then test their applicability on the spiritual precepts. That way it would be possible to reach a broad agreement on the process of our analysis or else we shall be caught up in the maze of discords right in the beginning.

1. Every action that we perform must have an equal and opposite reaction.
2. Nature performs all its functions with absolute impartiality and treats everyone as equal. It remains exactly the same for an ant, elephant and human being.
3. All natural phenomena and principles apply equally to all and sundry. Earth's gravitational pull is exactly the same for everything and everyone. Sun's rays fall on everybody with equal intensity. Variations if any, are not account of the sun, but are caused by factors like the distance, cloud cover and other local factors.
4. All living beings are subject to destruction and renewal.
5. All living entities have to perform work as long as they live. The need to work ceases only on death.
6. The cause of everything that happens to you must lie within you and not outside of you.

7. You are responsible for everything that happens to you and no one else can be blamed for it. It may either be on account of your own actions or you may have, by your own actions created certain conditions that have caused it.

These are all scientifically proven and tested precepts. It must be, as a further point of clarification added that the entire living organism is an integral part of nature, and the laws and principles that apply to nature must inevitably apply to all living entities as well. The most important principle that we need to remember is its neutrality and an absolute sense of justice. Everything else would thus fall in place.

We must now add to our analysis some facts that are based on scriptural knowledge. These are facts that can not be proved by any scientific analysis, but have been realized by some highly enlightened personages and must be treated as competent evidence. These experiences have been documented in our scriptures and are accepted as truths by all followers of that sect. There is nothing unusual about this. We know for sure that our sense perception has certain limitations and there is knowledge beyond senses, and if it does not contradict any past experience, it must be treated as proof. Also, if a person of absolutely impeccable credentials has experienced and documented it with conviction, we would gracefully accept it as proof.

Indian philosophy, Vedanta thought clearly describes this universe as one single entity with one master, who controls the creation, sustenance and destruction of the universe. That is the concept of Advaitvad, non-duality and subscribes to the view of an eternal existence of all living beings. It further divides the living entities into subtle and gross, and while treating the subtle component as eternal, creates a mechanism by which the gross lives its life for a stipulated period, dies and is renewed again. All this while, the subtle component remains as an integral part of the Supreme master or the energy. We traditionally define these entities as Atma and Parmatma.

1. All living beings are an integral part of that one single entity known as God.
2. Our true self is the soul which is pure, pristine and immortal.
3. We are in this world as His representatives, and our only objective in life is to go back to our origin. All our efforts and endeavours must be aimed at attaining Him.
4. One of the several ways to attain Him is through the instrumentality of good karmas.
5. Each of our karmas that comprise thought, speech and action will create an effect and we alone are the legitimate recipients of that effect. This is both spiritual fact and science.
6. Nature, whose chief attribute has been identified as impartial and just, will also ensure happening of this phenomenon.

Combination of the scientific and the spiritual postulates enumerated above and their joint reading, will lead to only one conclusion, and that will contain answers to some of the questions that often torment us.

We are permanent residents of this universe. Some part of our self, the gross part which in its very nature is subjected to decay, seeks constant regeneration and is therefore invisible for some time, and rejoins the subtle part of our being. While the subtle component is pure and eternal, and does not involve itself in any pursuits spiritual or temporal, the gross part is perennially engaged in performing karmas for survival and other material gains. It therefore, does all kinds of karmas under the influence of the three Gunas that are part of his nature. No living being in this universe is absolutely perfect, nor will any one person perform only good karmas all his life or several lives that he is ordained to live. Majority of people, either because of ignorance of their true calling in life or because of their complete identification with the gross, perform karmas that is a mix of good and evil. There are some who quickly realize their true goal and therefore, largely perform good karmas. A third category, completely convinced about the supremacy of their body and prevalence of destructive nature, performs karmas that cause only trouble to others. They live their life on their own terms and devise their own rules in utter disregard to the feeling and welfare of others. They tend to regard nature and the laws of nature as irrelevant.

Everyone shall be called upon to answer for their karmas. That is inevitable because karma is one part of the chain, of which effect is the other. It is also inextricably linked to the cause and effect syndrome which really is the basis of sustaining the universe in the form it exists. The entire universe is bound together by the force of energy which is generated by our karmas and other creations of nature, and each one is performing karmas perennially. This energy manifests itself in its impact on those who have performed the karmas as well as in causing new set of karmas. The cause and effect, karmas and their result is therefore, a perennial process that constantly produces that energy and expends it on a regular basis. All this as a part of natural phenomenon, gets evenly distributed to those who have performed the respective karmas. This is only fair and inevitable. Science and spirituality combine here to ensure that impact of karmas, good or bad shall have to be borne only by those who have performed them and none else. There is no law on this earth or any other planet that says that the effect of one person's karmas should be borne by another.

What appears to be unjust and iniquitous can only be explained by this process. Those enjoying good times, despite indulging in evil acts in this birth are really doing so on the basis of their past karmas, and once that has been exhausted or once the energy content of their good deeds is dissipated, they will cease to be wealthy and powerful. They are thereupon, visited by their negative balance of karmas and lead a miserable life. We have seen that happening in this life for many an individual. Once considered mighty, some have a terrible fall and end their life in an utterly miserable manner. Alternatively, those undergoing severe hardships without ostensibly committing evil acts are really going through the effects of their past deeds unknown and invisible to them, and having passed the test of their punishment and penance, they are ready to partake of the good times. This again is nothing unusual and is very much a part of the normal happenings that we observe in the world. Many with humble beginnings rise to unimaginable levels of great power and prosperity, only on account of their good deeds and karmas.

This is what Krishna meant when He described to Arjuna the phenomenon of life and death, as also the effect of their karmas. In Chapter 10, Shloka 21, He says the following:

Te Tvam Bhuktva Swaraglokam Vishalam
Khshine Punye Mritulokam Vishanti
Aivam Trayidharmam Anuprapanna
Gatagatam Kamkama Labhante

"Those desirous of material comforts, habitually perform karmas that bind them. Good karmas facilitate their enjoyment of the heavenly pleasures and once these have been frittered away, they go back to the world and undergo the travails of living".

Bottom line for all that has been described is the performance of karmas and nothing else. Our karmas have an influence on our habits and habits in a repetitive mode construct our nature which in turn, influences all our karmas. During the course of numerous lives that we live here, till we finally merge with our origin, we are subjected to two mandatory phenomena. Death, indeed several deaths to our gross part, is one of them and performance of karmas is another. Everything else is optional.

Death being a common denominator, the only other factor that is responsible for diverse and vastly different experiences that different human beings go through, has to be their karmas and nothing else.

Chapter 12

Life After Death

"All beings are mortal.
They are immortalized only through their karmas."

I should be quick to disabuse the minds of readers, who wish to be enlightened about what happens to all of us after death. This book is not intended to describe any supernatural or paranormal experience, indeed the author does not claim to have any knowledge of such phenomena. In fact, I firmly discount occurrence of any miracles or paranormal events and strongly believe that everything in this universe takes place on a rational and scientific basis. There is nothing in this world that happens without a cause. There is no such thing as being snatched from the jaws of death. The so called near-death experiences are only a figment of one's imagination. You are either dead or not and there is no condition in between, and any experience some people describe relating to coming back from the throes of death, must be dismissed as hallucinatory.

I am a strong proponent of erasing some of the words that have made an entry rather surreptitiously, into the English lexicon. These are accident, chance and destiny. These words indicate activity or phenomena that occur without any cause or reason and something that defies any rational explanation.

I have no hesitation in rubbishing this claim. Nothing in this universe happens without a cause and there is nothing in this universe that does not serve any purpose. God or any other supernatural entity cannot be accused of being engaged in creating events or beings that are utterly useless. Our ignorance about the purpose of that creation or the cause of an event is no ground for dismissing it as useless or irrelevant. Our knowledge of the various phenomena in the universe is acquired through the instrumentality of our sense-mind-intellect combination. These have their limitations, and one life is grossly inadequate to imbibe the entire water from the ocean of knowledge and wisdom. We have seven of them in this planet alone. All of us will do well by bowing before the infinite power and knowledge of the Master of the universe and acknowledge with great humility the following facts:

1. Our planet, indeed the entire universe is too huge and complex for us to understand all the phenomena that take place here.
2. We are only an infinitesimal part of this universe and in fact, an insignificant dot. It is however, possible to raise our level and power manifold, only on the strength of our karmas and enhance our knowledge quotient. There is no such thing as absolute knowledge which perhaps vests only, if at all, in only one entity, The God.
3. Every creation has a purpose, but there is nothing that is indispensable. None of the living beings fall in the category of the indispensable.
4. This world does not need us. We may need it though, for our survival.
5. The void caused by our departure from the world, or any other position is quickly filled in by someone else, who may be more competent.

6. Death causes only a temporary halt and everybody's life goes on and beyond a stage, even the memories start fading.
7. One death is only one insignificant event in the series of many births and deaths we are required to experience in our journey.
8. Let us not suffer from any delusions of immortality. None of us ever can achieve immortality. We have to visualize the difference between our identity or name, and the legacy of karmas that we leave behind. Immortality, if at all, can be lent only to our karmas.
9. All our karmas will stay and have an impact. We will cease to have any role to play after we are gone.

Mention must be made of a categorical and an unambiguous statement made by Krishna in Chapter 18 at Shlokas 5 and 6 which are as follows:

Yagya Daan Tapa Karma
Na Tyajyam Karyamev Tat
Yagyo Danam Tapa Cha Aiv
Pavnani Manishinam

"Yagya, charity and diligence in work must never be abandoned. All these three, bring about great purity amongst all wise people".

Aitani Api Tu Karmani
Sangam Tyaktva Phalani Cha
Kartvyani Iti Me Partha
Nishchitam Matam Utamam

"O Arjuna, Yagya, charity, hard work and all other assigned duties must be performed without any attachment with rewards. This is my true and firm opinion."

We all carry an earnest desire to be remembered after we are gone. This is sheer vanity. This world and the people inhabiting it may be gracious enough to forgive our misdeeds, but to expect them to remember us as a person, for a long period of time is just being vainglorious. We shall be remembered only for our good karmas and nothing else.

In any case to carry that desire and make an attempt to seek immortality is an exercise in utter futility. To those harbouring such a desire, the following lines from a famous poem of the celebrated poet of nineteenth century, Mirza Ghalib who was also the poet to the last Mughal Emperor Bahadur Shah Zafar may be referred:

Yeh Na Thi Hamari Kismet
Hue Mar Ke Ham Jo Ruswa
Hue Kyon Na Garke Dariya
Na Kabhi Janaza Uth Ta
Na Kahin Mazar Hota

"In my departure from this world, I would prefer to get dissolved in the water of a river. This would do away with the need of taking out my funeral procession, and to set up my tomb".

In the twilight of our life, some of us often nurse certain regrets for not having done few things that we always wanted to do if there was enough time for them. When we had the time, we were busy performing inessentials and kept postponing them to an "appropriate" occasion. That appropriate occasion never came and the precious time slipped by. The most common and notable example pertains to spiritual pursuits, that some of us want to pursue. Essentially because of its inessential nature, we fail to do anything about it, hoping to engage ourselves in our old age. Old age, in our perception never comes and we miss the opportunity of remembering our lord, despite best of intentions. Some of us are also bitten by the charity bug and for paying back to society and the environment. These are all optional activities and our undue occupation with material desires and "important" matters of state prevent us from doing what all of us should be doing as part of our essential duties. Not doing these things, do not involve any sanctions, nor do they affect our engagements in the affairs of the world. We experience a sense of comfort in doing things that are familiar to us, and spending time in activities that we have never done becomes painful. We therefore, end up missing them altogether. Then death suddenly strikes and we leave this world without doing anything worthwhile, and of course, not doing something that we want to do.

If you want to do something good, or something that you think you should, do not wait for the suitable opportunity. Just do it and do it now. One must remember that for performing an evil act, or for wasting precious moments of your life, it does not require much effort. You can remain idle and waste you precious moments, but for achieving and indeed, doing something worthwhile, you shall have to make a conscious effort. It will not happen on its own. Death for all of us is lurking somewhere around the corner, close by. Let us not have any regrets for a life not fully lived.

In order to perform good karmas, we shall have to initiate the process. These will not happen without the requisite effort on our part. Good karmas require a positive frame of mind and determination to fight evil forces within. In the beginning, our efforts in this direction may generate some resistance from both within us, as well as from the person we are likely to benefit. Persistence shall be essential and you will discover unimaginable bliss after having done it.

Krishna gave a beautiful and profound description of actions or karmas that are cause of permanent bliss in Shloka 37 in Chapter 18 as follows:

Yatdagre Visham Iv
Pariname Amritopamam
Tatsukham Satvikam Proktam
Atmabudhi Prasadjam

"Something that tastes like poison in the beginning is like nectar in its effect. That provides permanent bliss and is pure food for intellect and our soul".

All pleasant things that attract our senses are harmful and conversely, all good and positive actions and karmas taste like a medicinal pill, but relieve a person of his pain and misery and act like nectar.

Let us resolve to live our life to the fullest. Zest for life should be evident in full flow in all our actions. Let us consciously perform karmas that are naturally good. We must ensure full care of our body and mind, their health and soundness, must give complete protection to those who are dependent on us, and at the same time spare adequate efforts in service of others. We must seek to live our life within the means that we have earned legitimately on the strength of our own efforts, and diligently avoid borrowing it from others to enhance our own comfort levels. If in some contingency, we have borrowed something from others, we must as quickly as possible, return it to its original owner with interest and compliments. Make sure that you do not die with any debt and do not expect others to discharge it.

Apart from some material debts, we also owe debts to earth, nature and the Supreme lord for giving us all that we got, however little during our life that we spent on this planet. This class of debt shall never be demanded unlike the material one, but the burden of discharging is no less essential.

The phenomenon relating to our life and death will continue unabated till we reach a level, again on the strength of our karmas when we are released from its bondage. The universe however, will continue to remain and verily, play host to our several lives and deaths in the meanwhile. The kind of life we spend will necessarily impact this universe in diverse ways. Most of us are net borrowers from this universe, reducing the overall content of cosmic energy that must remain here for the universe's operation and maintenance. This gap has to be filled in by nature's own resources or by celestial objects. Over a period of time, this would become unsustainable and impact the purity and the pristine nature of the universe and its perennial prized possessions. There is thus a broad environmental issue involved which bears a close relationship with our karmas. Our evolutionary movement in this universe therefore, must be guided by this truth.

We will keep visiting this earth, be part of this universe many times over, and would certainly not want to see it in a state inferior to what we saw it last time around. In order to ensure this, we shall have to consider the following:

1. Let us learn to treat the entire universe, as one entity and the world as one family. "Vasudevam Kuttumbkam" is the phrase used by Vedanta thought to describe this.
2. Our evolutionary march in this planet shall have to be based on the principles of cooperation and not in the spirit of competition. We end up using and indeed, wasting precious natural resources when we compete. The spirit of cooperation will help us pool our resources and save on them, extending the longevity of the universe in its pristine state. When we work with the spirit of cooperation, we are empathetic to the needs of one another. We share wealth in proportion to the effort or the capital an individual has put in. We also willingly

exchange best practices. Everybody in the cooperative system becomes a responsible member of the family and in a family you do not create any conflict of interest.

3. Competition creates tensions and each stakeholder tries to corner to himself, the maximum benefits often to the detriment of others. Cooperation is an inclusive method where everyone partakes of the cake in proportion to his requirement, whereas competition leaves out many deserving people from the growth cycle. Most importantly, cooperation ensures an optimum exploitation of resources, both natural and man-made.
4. Death as a common denominator must be reckoned as an important factor to bring all residents of this planet to work together in the spirit of cooperation.
5. Conscious awareness of death will also create a sense of urgency in completing whatever task we wish to accomplish in this short life. Taken in its right spirit, it will also help to remove any sense of complacency and tendency to procrastinate.
6. Pay back either directly or through the people inhabiting this planet, whatever you have taken from here for your own use.

In the words of famous Sufi poet Kabir:

Ye Chadder Sab Nar Muni Orhi
Orh Ke Maili Keeni
Das Kabir Jatan Se Orhi
Jyon Ki Tyon Dhar Deeni Chadariya

"While everyone else was busy messing up with nature and its resources, Kabir replaced all his earthly belongings in the same state that he had taken and caused no harm".

Please remember that we came into this world empty handed, and go back we must in the same state.

Epilogue

Death and birth, in a way are the two sides of a coin and are inseparable.

They are also likened to the two wheels of a chariot and are essential for the smooth movement of the universe, and maintain it in youthful and pristine form.

Death is a renewal and hence a celebration.

Let us live our life to the fullest so that there is no regret of having lived it inadequately.

Every moment is precious and must be savoured like every morsel of the food that we imbibe to lead a healthy and fulfilling life.

Let us not look upon death in any obsessive way, nor wait for it.

Accept it as inevitable, either as an end or as a beginning of another inning.

Index

BOOKS OF RELATED INTEREST

Celebrating Death: Life after Death—Beginning or End?—***Dr. Jonn Mumford***

Discover the ultimate truth about death. This book is an exhilarating celebration of life and death. Explore the history of death rituals and attitudes from other ages and cultures, and uncover surprising facts about this inevitable life event. This thought-provoking and interactive book will alter your perceptions about death and prepare you for reincarnation.

Rights: South-east Asia • 197 pages, 20x30x8, 2004 • ***978-81-7822-155-7***

The Definitive Dream Dictionary—***Diane Bellchambers***

This book is the ultimate reference tool to help you unlock the meanings of your dreams. This contemporary, self teaching guide empowers the dreamer, to ask the right questions and shows you how to link dream meanings to events taking place in your life, with more than 1700 symbols organised into commonsense chapters and an easy reference index.

Rights: Indian Subcontinent • 356 pages, 23x36x16, 2006 • ***978-81-7822-267-7***

The Great Mystery of Life Beyond Death—***Prof. Hiralal L. Kaji***

The varied experiences which a spirit undergoes after death are described in this book with clarity and verisimilitude, giving the reader a rare glimpse of another, unknown dimension.

The book makes fascinating reading and will certainly provide food for thought, even for the most hardened sceptic.

Rights: World • 175 pages, 23x36x16, 2003 • ***978-81-7822-138-0***

The Web of Life: Life force: The Energetic Constitution of Man and the Neuro-Endocrine—***John Davidson***

The author understands and acknowledges the advancements made in the field of biological sciences but is not satisfied with them. He points out the shortcomings in the approach of science and tries to rectify them. He provides a new conceptual framework for the further advancement of science and the healing arts.

Rights: World • 408 pages, 23x36x16, 2010 • ***978-81-7822-346-9***

Psychic Powers A Practical Guide—Awaken Your Sixth Sense—**Melita Denning & Osborne Phillips**

This practical guide offers complete step-by-step instructions on developing your innate psychic skills in divination, dowsing, clairvoyance, psychometry, and spirit communication. You will learn now to safely enhance your mental and psychic abilities, and to use your abilities to positively change your life and the lives of those around you.

Rights: South-east Asia • B/W Illustrations • 215 pages, 23x36x16, 2002 • ***978-81-7822-051-2***

The Encyclopedia of Dream Interpretation—***Eili Goldberg***

This encyclopedia is a collection of interpretations of thousands of dreams and dream fragments. The author examined 73 different dream dictionaries and countless other books dealing with dreams and their meanings. This impressive encyclopedia is unique in that it both interprets the dream and relates to dreams as an important tool to access and understand the entire consciousness and personality of the dreamer.

Rights: Indian Subcontinent • 1039 pages, 23x36x16, 2009 • ***978-81-7822-348-3***